Financial Wellness

The Guide to Financial Security, Growth, Preservation and Fulfillment

Financial Wellness

The Guide to Financial Security, Growth, Preservation and Fulfillment

Table of Contents

∞

Chapter 1

About the Program

When I was thirty-three-years-old, I set a goal that I wanted to have a net worth of a million dollars by the time I turned forty. I wrote the goal down in a letter and showed it to a few people. I then quietly went to work to make it a reality.

Having the benefit of a finance degree and an MBA helped me achieve my financial goal. The formal classroom training did give me the confidence to strike out on my own after college. Contrary to some critics of higher education, I am happy to report that what I learned in the classroom did help in the real world.

General accounting and finance principles came in handy in running my own business. Knowing how to read an income statement and a balance sheet and keeping my eye on the bottom line was paramount to the business success that I've enjoyed.

Another thing that helped me is I adopted the habit of reading personal development books. Great books such as "Think and Grow Rich" by Napoleon Hill and "The Magic of Thinking Big" by David Schwartz got me excited and motivated to keep going during times of uncertainty.

I learned that times change, and we must adapt to the new normal. I learned that change is not bad but rather it can be a great opportunity. A great book to read on how to respond to change is "Who Moved My Cheese" by Dr. Spencer Johnson.

In fact, I think that to grow, there must be change. Therefore, our future success in attaining our goals requires that something be different. So, the more comfortable we are with it, the more opportunities we will encounter and be able to act upon.

For me, I was able reach my financial goals in a large way with a combination of owning my own businesses and investing in real estate and the stock market. But as I think about it, I believe it really came down to three all important principles of attaining any goal in life: having the right attitude, setting the goal, and taking action.

That is why when I speak about having financial wellness, I make sure that I include these three all important components from the beginning. It's one of those principles in life that without getting them right from the start, financial wellness may prove to be an elusive target that we just can't ever seem to hit.

Make no mistake I also have to give credit where credit is due. I grew up in a large family of eight kids in a home that was very stable with great parents.

Since our family was so large and didn't have a high income, we qualified for reduced lunches at school. This was a little embarrassing in the school cafeteria, but so what? It helped me learn the value of a dollar.

I paid for college by living at home for a couple of years (thanks Mom and Dad!) working through school and with help of a Pell Grant from the government.

When I graduated, I had no money. After many interviews I was offered a job in Lafayette, LA., which I was very glad to accept even though I had no idea where that was. The country was in a recession at the time because of the savings and loan crisis. No good finance jobs were available close to home.

I am especially grateful of that first job because it led me to where I met my wife. Funny how things work out! My point is that I was not handed many so-called advantages of wealth but benefited greatly by being taught good values while growing up. Before we go any further, let's explore these essential principles right now.

The Attitude

The Goal

The Action

∞

Chapter 2

The Attitude

Have you heard the phrase that attitude is everything? Having a great attitude is definitely 90% of what will take us through the inevitable obstacles that we all encounter along the road to our dream goal. This is true whether we are in search of financial peace of mind or any other goal that is big and worthwhile.

The reason that the right attitude is so important in our quest for financial wellness is that we have to make sure that our personal psychology of wealth is in line with our financial goals. We are not going to get very far if we have a dysfunctional or incongruent idea of what wealth really means to us.

This is because 90% of our personal wealth creation comes from our own way of thinking. We have to accept that we are the answer to solving the money mystery in our lives. In other words, we are responsible for the creation of wealth in our lives.

We own that. We have to realize that our financial freedom is not going to come from something outside of us. We have to say to ourselves, "If it's meant to be, it's up to me."

For example, our financial wellness is not going to come from our employer. It is not going to come from a benevolent family member or friend. It is not going to just fall in our lap someday from being lucky.

Our personal wealth is going to come in part from us adding value in the world. This is especially true in the beginning of our financial lives when we start to accumulate money through a chosen career path.

If there is one thing that can make the difference between really having a life free of financial worries and one where money seems to be a reoccurring problem, it has to be our own attitude. Thus the saying, "attitude is everything!" And even though that expression may be over-exaggerating a bit, it does make the point as to how important our attitude really is. In achieving financial wellness, can it be any other way? I certainly don't think so!

As we explore the concept of financial wellness in our lives, we may find that happiness is as much a state of mind as it is our actual personal net worth. In other words, our emotional well-being and psychology surrounding our finances is just as valuable to keep in perspective as keeping track and accounting for our investment growth and performance.

There's a story I heard once about a man who was traveling on a ship crossing the open ocean when they ran into a huge storm. The huge waves bashed and overflowed on the boat. The crew began to fear for their lives, and the captain ordered all unnecessary supplies be thrown overboard to lighten the boat so it wouldn't sink.

Well, this man was traveling with all his life's savings of valuable coins in a wooden chest. When two of the sailors grabbed the chest and heaved it overboard, the man jumped in after the chest. As the chest full of coins sank down and down, the man held on to it and perished.

The moral of the story is: Did the man have money and wealth, or did money and wealth have him? Yes, we want to have money and wealth because they have the potential to make our lives more comfortable and more fulfilling.

We instinctively know that having resources we own and control is a great benefit in life. I mean we all know that life is unpredictable, and we want to be safe.

This is true. However we want to maintain that we are the master and keep money and wealth in its proper perspective. Part of having the proper psychology of wealth is that our money is never more important than our physical and emotional well-being. Sure, money is important but there are other things in life much more important than that.

Our attitude in seeking financial wellness should be to do our best in our financial lives, but always keep it in balance with the other parts of our life that are, quite frankly, much more fulfilling. We'll talk much more about these other fulfilling areas of our lives later in the book.

∞

Chapter 3

The Goal

Do you wonder why most people have a hard time reaching their financial goals? I think I know why!

Most people have goals, but they don't have the tools to help them get past the thinking stage. It's one thing to think about accomplishing something, but it is quite another to actually follow the many little steps that it takes to reach those goals.

If it was easy to reach financial independence everybody would already be there, right? But the truth is, it's not easy to be financially well.

Even if we had several million bucks that wouldn't automatically mean that we are financially at peace. It might even lead to the direct opposite of financial wellness!

There are many reasons for this that we will cover later. However, all is not lost. The fact is that many people are able to reach financial wellness, and I'm going to show you how they do it and how you can achieve your personal version of being financially content.

Let me give an example of what I mean about some of the obstacles that present themselves to us on a day to day basis and that most people are not prepared for or even aware of the affects on our financial future. If you have a room full of people and you ask, "How many people in here have a goal?" You're going to get pretty much everyone in the room raising their hands because of course everybody does have a goal of one kind or another, right? I know because I've done this in real life at a seminar I used to give.

If you ask, "Of those people who have their hands up, how many have written down their goal?" Half the hands will go down because many people have their goal in their heads, but they haven't taken the time to think it out and write it down on paper.

Then you ask "Of those that still have their hands up, how many can find where they wrote down their goal?" In other words, is it someplace that they find it and can read it whenever they want?

If you ask the few that still have their hands up, "How many of you read your goal every day, or at least once a week?" Everyone will usually have their hands down by now.

Not a single hand is still in the air! If you really think about it, it's a sad event that we've just witnessed. We have in effect, discovered one of the main reasons why people don't reach their goals. It's not because their goals aren't realistic or they don't really care about their goals.

If you asked each one of those good people in the room if they had a serious goal that really meant a lot to them, they would say absolutely that it did mean a lot to them. The reason that people don't hit goals they set for themselves is because they don't have a good internal communication system to making those dreams come true.

If we can't communicate our goal to our subconscious minds on a regular basis then it's not a goal, it's wishful thinking. And how many dreams come true if they are simply wishful thinking?

Realistically, the challenge we all have is how do we follow through on our goals? And in this topic of financial wellness, how do we follow through on our financial goals? This book shows you the system I've used to help me follow and complete my goals and dreams.

The system is so simple you may almost dismiss it as being too simplistic. However, that's the reason that it works. It's simple, but the real power comes from it also being very personal.

The system I am talking about is using a goal card. On this goal card, we write down the date that we want to have our goal achieved by and the goal that we want to make a reality in our life.

The key here is to begin our first sentence by stating, "I am so happy and grateful now that..." at the beginning of our written goal. Follow this beginning by writing your goal as having already achieved it. In other words, we are saying that we are so happy and grateful that we already achieved our goal.

For example: "I am so happy and grateful now that I am living in my new home in the neighborhood where my family has always wanted to live and near the schools that we have always wanted to attend."

For the goal card, the more emotional words that we use the better. Remember, this is our burning desire. The more meaningful descriptions we use for our goal the better. What happens when we read this to ourselves is that we are communicating with our subconscious mind.

Our subconscious doesn't have the ability to reject ideas, only to accept what we feed it. Since our goal card is written in the present tense, our subconscious doesn't know any different and so it will go to work to create it in reality.

Our subconscious mind controls 95% of our daily lives. Thus, it's a very good thing for it to be in tune with what our goals are in life. By reading our goal card every day, we are letting our control center know that this is what's important to us right now.

Therefore our thoughts, decisions, and actions will be in tune with our overall goal. This is how we overcome the problem of life getting in the way of what's really important to us on a personal level.

All the clutter we get during the day can very easily overwhelm us and make us forget what we really want. This happens daily, and those days turn into months, and then into years. Using our goal card, we're using a simple to use tool that will keep us focused on what's important.

I have a portable and practical "Goal Card" that you can use to write down your goal and keep it with you at all times. This way you can read your goal every day and keep it in the fore-front of your mind.

Then, and only then, will your subconscious mind go to work to help you manifest your dreams and help you along your path to financial wellness. Send me an email from my web site (www.jbresnahan.com), and I'll mail you a goal card for free.

∞

Chapter 4

The Action

Once we have our goal and the right attitude, we are ready to take action. This book on financial wellness is definitely an action-oriented guide.

It's only through taking action that we can actually accomplish our fulfilling life. We are as capable of achieving our desires as much as anyone else. This book will help you build the habits that financially successful people have.

Let's begin the journey by having the correct habits that will set you free financially. Why? Because these habits of taking the right actions will make you master of your own financial destiny and give you the resources to live a life of great personal fulfillment.

A truly wonderful lesson that I've learned is that once we decide to take a certain action, other things begin to happen that help us along toward our goal. These helpful aids we could never have planned on or thought of ahead of time. They come along only after we've made our decision to make our move, and we begin to take action toward our goal.

This assistance is spiritual in nature, and we have to be open to it or we may dismiss it when it does come our way. The following quote by Johann Goethe, a German philosopher from more than 200 years ago, describes this very same phenomenon that I believe in so strongly.

> "Until one is committed, there is hesitancy, the chance to draw back, always ineffectiveness. Concerning all acts of initiative there is one elementary truth, the ignorance of which kills countless ideas and endless plans: That the moment one definitely commits oneself, then providence moves, too.
>
> "All sorts of things occur to help one that would never otherwise have occurred. A whole stream of events issues from the decision, raising in one's favor all manner of material assistance which no man could have dreamed would come his way. Whatever you can do or dream you can, begin it! Boldness has genius, power, and magic in it."
>
> Johann Goethe

To begin taking action on our way to financial freedom, take a moment here to make a decision and commit to it. Please read the commitment to your family below out loud then sign and date it.

My commitment to my family's financial wellness:

"I am committed to take the necessary daily steps to ensure that my spending and saving habits are in line with the goals and dreams that I want to realize for me and my family. The importance of this commitment is above anything else in my life."

Signature: _____

Date: _____

∞

Chapter 5

Financial Wellness:
The Four Baskets

Now that we have discussed the importance of having a balanced attitude about money, setting goals and taking action, let's move on to the specifics. There are four baskets in the Financial Wellness life plan.

These are the keys to financial freedom:

☆ **Security**
☆ **Growth**
☆ **Preservation**
☆ **Fulfillment**

Security is something that we all have programmed in us already at birth. We want to take care of ourselves. It's part of our survival mechanism as human beings.

Therefore, it is the foundation upon which we start building our financial wellness. The success of your future financial well-being depends on getting this security basket off to a good start.

After we get our security in place, **growth** is the engine that will produce the momentum needed to accumulate the wealth we want for our current and future life. This basket is where we will spend the majority of our time and energy because time spent here is measured in years.

In fact, the longer we spend here, the more wealth we will be able to create for ourselves and our families. The sooner we get started in the growth basket the better.

After a while of being in the growth basket we will want to begin putting some of our profits in our **preservation** basket. This is the basket that we will be drawing our income from during our later years when we aren't working for a living. As we are living longer as a society, we want to make sure that our preservation basket is set up and made to last.

Our **fulfillment** is the pinnacle of our financial wellness. Our fulfillment basket is at the end of the list however, it certainly isn't the least.

None of the baskets are more important than any other. Rather they all work in unison to accomplish our overall goals. Fulfillment is something that we can enjoy throughout life, from the beginning to the very end.

∞

Chapter 6

Basket #1 – Security

The security basket is filled with everyday living necessities such as: our home, insurance, short term savings for living expenses, and savings for emergencies. It's also our car, furniture, food, health care, and things that we need to live our life on a daily basis. Checking and savings accounts, credit cards, and money market accounts are the tools we'll use here to begin building our financial wellness.

The goal in the security basket is to protect the survival of ourselves and our family with the basics. This basket isn't going to provide for extravagant living, not much luxury, not much for big emergencies or medical expenses, not much for college education, and not much for a high quality retirement. This basket simply takes care of our needs for the here and now.

That's not to say that this isn't an important basket, or as important as the other baskets, not at all. This is the beginning! This is the starting point!

This is the foundation of all the financial wellness that we will experience for the rest of our lives. So in many ways, all the other baskets depend upon this hugely important basket.

The other baskets won't have much in them if this security basket is not acted upon at some point in our lives. The sooner we get our security basket right, the sooner we can get on with building up our other baskets. Getting our security basket right means following some simple philosophies!

Feeling secure and safe is one of the most basic instincts that we have. To begin with, let's define security. We can define it in general terms so that it will apply to most people because security is a subjective term that will mean different things to different people.

Security is both a feeling and a reality. And yet they're not the same. The feeling of security comes from having a pretty good idea that everything is as it should be and that there won't be any negative surprises coming down the road that we can't handle. This feeling of being safe depends on our individual personality and background, so it will be different for everyone.

Security is also a reality in the sense that we have actually taken care of the threats that we face in our daily lives. For example, we may live in a low crime area so statistically we are safe because the chance of something bad happening to us or our family is very low. Therefore, we take steps to ensure that mathematically and realistically, we are secure in addition to our feeling safe and secure.

This is the same approach to achieving the first step in financial wellness. It can be called the first rule to financial freedom. We want to realistically be secure in addition to feeling secure.

To accomplish this, we'll want to take care of ourselves and our families in a financially secure way. Begin a habit of saving money. If we don't already have this habit, it's always best to start a new habit by taking small steps so we don't overwhelm ourselves and give up before the habit sticks. Let's assume that we don't have a good savings habit and go through some scenarios of how to begin the habit of saving money.

> "The philosophy of the rich versus the poor is this: The rich invest their money and spend what is left over; the poor spend their money and invest what is left."
>
> *Jim Rohn*

Before we talk too much about how to save money, let's talk about why it's important first. Why is saving money such a big deal?

Aren't there important things in our lives that are a lot more fun to do and talk about? Isn't money supposed to be spent and not hoarded?

Saving money is important because if we don't, we may spend it on things that don't last, and we'll never have the chance to accumulate any wealth for bigger things later. Remember, we aren't talking about saving all our money, but we are talking about saving some. I suggest saving at minimum 10% to 15% of the income, and 20% is better.

Another important reason to save money early on in our lives is because of the power of compounding. This power of compounding is in effect our money working for us.

Yes, through the power of compounding of interest, our money is working for us and earning us more money, even while we sleep. Eventually, our money will be earning enough that we won't have to work anymore. We'll just let our money do the work, and we can focus on other more important things.

That sounds great, right? However, that will absolutely never happen if we spend all our income. That won't happen if we don't put some of our income into savings so that it will begin to grow.

We have to start and keep feeding our savings account. If we do this, the power of compounding will go to work for us.

A habit of saving makes all this much easier. And easier is what we want. Also, keep in mind that while it's getting easier, it's also getting more fun. As saving money becomes fun, it becomes a habit, and that's how we're going to build our security basket.

If you are having a hard time saving money and don't know where to begin, here is a list of ten ideas. They won't all apply, of course, but the idea is to pick some that you don't do currently and start adopting them to your routine. Remember, one or two ideas to begin with are all we want to come up with at this point:

A Dollar Saved is a Dollar Earned

1. Give up or cut down on expensive habits: cigarettes, alcohol, golf, gourmet coffee, elegant dining, etc.

2. Be diligent about turning off lights before you leave. If we spend one minute turning off lights before a two-hour trip, that's the equivalent of earning $50 an hour.

3. Borrow books from the library instead of buying new ones.

4. Drink water at restaurants instead of ordering drinks. Water is healthier, and it's free.

5. Switch to term life insurance. It's less expensive than whole life for the same amount of coverage.

6. Wash your own car instead of taking it to a car wash. It can also be a fun family event.

7. When you buy a car plan on keeping it for ten years.

8. Wash and iron your clothes instead of taking them to the cleaners.

9. Mow the yard instead of hiring a company to do it.

10. Quit the expensive gym membership if you hardly ever use it and take walks or jog with a neighbor.

Target Number

Having a habit of saving money is probably the most important part of building up our security basket. This can be easier said than done depending on our personality.

One way to get started is to set a goal of building up a savings account equal to six months of living expenses. This is a good idea because it forces us to begin thinking about how much our living expenses are in the first place.

The best way to determine what our actual expenses are is to plug them into a budget (see budget worksheet example to follow). This worksheet will give us a monthly expense number that we can use to set our goal of six months of living expenses.

Once we have a target number, it makes saving for it so much easier because we have something measureable to shoot for. We'll know when we put money into savings that it's building up, and we will eventually hit our target.

The following budget example is for a fictitious couple John and Jane Doe that have an income of around $115,000 per year. Their yearly expenses are less than that, so it leaves them with about 16% of their income available to save and invest for the year. This 16% is about $18,000 which is great if they actually follow through with the habit of investing it for the future and not spending it today.

Sample Budget Worksheet

Monthly Living Expenses Section

Description	Current Budget	Current Actual	Difference
LIFESTYLE EXPENSES	-	-	-
Food			
Groceries	$600	$700	-$100
Dining	$200	$150	$50
Other			$0
Total food	$800	$850	-$50
Clothing			
Clothing and Shoes	$200	$175	$25
Cleaning, laundry			$0
Jewelry, watches, etc.			$0
Other			$0
Total clothing	$200	$175	$25
Housing (excluding mortgage and other debt)			
Real estate taxes	$1,350	$1,350	$0
Insurance	$140	$140	$0
Furniture and furnishings	$50	$100	-$50
Appliances	$0	$50	-$50
Repairs and maintenance	$30	$0	$30
Cleaning, laundry	$180	$180	$0
Electricity	$290	$300	-$10
Gas	$100	$75	$25
Heating	$0	$0	$0
Water and sewer	$135	$120	$15
Telephone	$176	$150	$26
Cable	$110	$110	$0
Other			$0

Total housing	$2,561	$2,575	-$14
Personal			
Personal care and toiletries	$20	$30	-$10
Child care			$0
Life Insurance	$45	$45	$0
Disability insurance			$0
Other			$0
Total personal	$65	$75	-$10
Medical			
Doctors, dentists and hospitals	$30	$50	-$20
Medicine	$20	$0	$20
Health Insurance			$0
Other			$0
Total medical	$50	$50	$0
Transportation (excluding debt)			
Repairs and maintenance	$40	$50	-$10
Insurance	$120	$120	$0
Gas, oil and tires	$300	$275	$25
Public transportation			$0
Other			$0
Total transportation	$460	$445	$15
Charity			
Religious Organizations	$100	$100	$0
Education Organizations	$20	$0	$20
Other	$150	$150	$0
Total charity	$270	$250	$20
Miscellaneous			
Books, magazines and newspapers	$15	$15	$0
Vacations	$420	$450	-$30
Entertainment	$10	$20	-$10
Clubs		$125	-$125
Education			$0
Legal			$0
Accounting			$0
Gifts Given			$0

Other			$0
Total miscellaneous	$445	$610	-$165
TOTAL LIFESTYLE EXPENSES	$4,851	$5,030	-$179
OTHER EXPENSES (OPTIONAL)			
Home Mortgage	$1,550	$1,550	$0
Auto Debt			$0
Other Debt Payments			$0
Income Taxes	$1,500	$1,500	$0
Other			$0
TOTAL OTHER EXPENSES	$3,050	$3,050	$0
TOTAL MONTHLY EXPENSES	$7,901	$8,080	-$179
TOTAL ANNUAL EXPENSES	$94,812	$96,960	-$2,148

Monthly Income Section

Description	Current Actual
INCOME SOURCES	-
Unemployment Insurance	
Total Unemployment	$0
Severance Pay	
Total Severance	$0
Social Security Benefits	
Total Social Security	$0
Pension	
From Previous Job	$10,000
Total Pension	$10,000
Full Time/Temporary Jobs	
John	$55,000

Jane	$50,000
Total Full Time/Temp Jobs	$105,000
Misc. Income Ex: Yard Sale	
Total Misc. Income	$0
TOTAL ANNUAL INCOME	$115,000
TOTAL MONTHLY INCOME	$9,583
ANNUAL SAVINGS AMOUNT	$18,040
ANNUAL SAVINGS %	16%

Note: If you want a "blank" budget worksheet for yourself visit www.jbresnahan.com and send me an email asking for one. I'll be happy to give one to you.

Debt Management

One of the financial wellness rules to building a security basket that will be a firm foundation for future wealth is to pay off any credit card debt before we begin to add to a savings account. The reason is that it's just simple math. Credit cards seem to charge anywhere from 9% to 30% (I don't really know how high some of them can go, I just know it is a lot more than anyone should be paying).

There is no way that we are going to earn that kind of return on our savings. Therefore, the easy math is if we pay down the debt each month, it's as if we are earning that 9% to 30% on our money. The only difference is that our money is paying down a debt instead of earning interest in a savings account.

When we pay off our credit card debt, begin putting the same amount of money, or more, into a savings or money market account. This strategy will also give us the added benefit of peace of mind knowing that our debt is taken care of and it's not hanging over our head any longer making us worried and depressed.

You may be asking yourself, "If this works with credit card debt, does it also work with other kinds of debt such as school loans, car loans, home loans, and other debts?" The answer is it depends. How high is the interest rate that you are paying on these other loans?

All we have to do is apply the same simple math. If the interest on the loan is higher than the interest that we would be getting from our savings accounts, then we pay off the loan first.

A restriction to this simple math may come for those saving to buy a home. Our financial wellness plan should account for a home mortgage payment because we should begin saving before we buy a home.

You should be saving every month at least the amount needed to pay a monthly mortgage payment on the home that you want. In addition, you should have anywhere from 5% to 20% of the price of the prospective home in savings so that you can use it for the initial down payment.

By putting 20% down we can avoid paying the Private Mortgage Insurance (PMI) premiums. This is insurance that lenders require when buying a home with less than the 20% down. This insurance protects the lenders in case the homeowner can't make the mortgage payments.

If you don't have the 20% to pay down on the home in the beginning, it's all right, but you should plan on catching up as soon as you can by making extra payments on the loan. Once you reach the 20% equity in the home's value, you can request the lender to take the PMI off your loan and lower your payment.

If you already bought your home, go back to the simple math test of determining whether you should either make extra payments to pay down a home loan with a high interest rate, get a better return by paying off another higher interest bearing debt, or invest the money in something better. The basic idea of where to put your extra income is based on the simple math of what's the highest return.

Remember, here in the United States, we do get a federal deduction on our income taxes for the interest portion on the home loan. Therefore, the actual cost of the interest we are paying is a little less than the stated rate because we get some back as a tax deduction. The amount of your deduction depends on the tax bracket you're in for federal income tax purposes. See the following example:

Given:

Home Loan Amount: $100,000
Interest Rate on Home Loan: 7%
Personal Tax Bracket: 28%

Solution:

Interest Paid During the Year: $100,000 x 7% = $7,000
Potential Income Tax Deduction Savings: $7,000 x 28% = $1,960
Actual Interest Paid After Deduction: $7,000 - $1,960 = $5,040
Actual Interest Rate After Deduction: $5,040/$100,000 = 5%

From the example above, after deduction of the benefit the government gives us for being home owners, our cost for having this home loan went from 7% to 5% given that we are paying income taxes at the 28% rate. If our income tax rate is higher than 28%, the savings is even more. If our annual income tax rate is lower than 28%, the difference will be less.

If the example above were your situation, and you think that you can earn better than 5% on an investment then you should be investing your money and not pay down the home loan. Also, if other debts exist that have a higher interest rate than 5%, pay those debts off first.

Use the formula above to figure your own actual after tax mortgage interest rate. It's a good thing to know for making your decisions of where to place your available investment dollars.

Give the gift of delayed gratification to yourself. It is a gift and one that will pay you great dividends many times over.

Insurance

Life and possibly disability insurance is another must to consider when building the security basket. This is especially true when dependents count on your income for their livelihood.

Life Insurance

Life insurance is really quite inexpensive now compared to what it used to be just a few years ago. The reason is that life expectancy has gone up for both men and women.

For men it is in the low 80s and for women it is in the high 80s, so 85 is about the average. If we are healthy, it's not uncommon to live well into our 90s. It is said that babies born in this century have a good chance of living to one-hundred-years-old. This is because of the advances in medicine and technology and the trend is expected to continue.

This is very much part of the benefit of modern health care and control of deadly diseases that not too long ago used to take lives at an earlier age. Polio affected my father when he was young, and although he lived, he had some friends that did not make it.

Now there's a vaccine that has almost completely eradicated this disease from the globe. Smallpox has also been eliminated from the world. Some types of cancer and diabetes can be brought under control with medications.

These and other examples of once deadly diseases have been controlled which means longer lives in general. Therefore, the cost of insuring people to offer protection for an early demise has gone down.

Term insurance is the least expensive and offers great life insurance protection. There is also permanent life insurance that offers a savings vehicle along with the life insurance called a cash value.

I bought a permanent life policy when my first son was born fifteen years ago. This same policy has earned enough cash value through the savings vehicle that it is all but self-sustaining.

This means that the dividends that the policy has earned pay the annual insurance premium for me. I still get the insurance, but I don't have to pay for it anymore because the policy itself is paying for it.

There are several types of life insurance. You will want to either talk to an insurance professional to get all the facts, or keep it simple and buy term insurance. Term is probably what I would recommend in most cases because it is the least expensive and a person can take the savings from the lower premiums and invest them in a conservative growth strategy in an IRA account. The benefit is that we have the control of the investments not some insurance company.

With life insurance, your heirs pay no income tax on the proceeds. Therefore, a $500,000 policy delivers $500,000 in benefits with no deductions and no withholding required. Note: This is true with all life insurance policies, both term and cash value.

You can avoid potential estate taxes and probate costs on policy proceeds, as long as the beneficiary designations and policy ownership are arranged in accordance with current law. For instance, if you (A) own your policy at the time of your death or (B) make your estate the beneficiary, the policy proceeds will generally be included in your estate at death.

This can increase the value of your estate, triggering estate taxes. This situation may be avoided, however, by placing ownership and naming beneficiaries outside your estate.

If structured properly, the policy proceeds will not be included in your estate. However, to avoid estate inclusion for existing policies, the policy must be transferred more than three years before your death. Consult your tax and legal advisors regarding your particular circumstances.

Advantages of Term Life Insurance

Simplicity

Planning financial goals around a cash value insurance plan can get really complicated. There are non-trivial rules governing things like the size of your cash value savings versus the policy death benefit, and the repayment of policy loans. Term life, on the other hand, is the essence of simplicity. Pay the premium, get covered for the term.

Competitive pricing

Because they are so simple, term life policies can be easily compared on the basis of price. This has led to a very competitive market in which term life policies are rapidly becoming a commodity.

Flexibility

Many term life policies are both "renewable" and "convertible." The former insures that you can re-up for another term policy without a medical exam. The latter allows you to convert your term life policy into an equivalent cash value policy from the same carrier, should this make sense during the term of the policy.

Advantages of Permanent Life Insurance

Forced savings

By moving some savings contributions into a bill that must be paid, your premium payment, cash value plans do promote the savings habit. However, automatic payroll deductions into a tax-sheltered retirement account can serve the same purpose.

Also, funds can be automatically and regularly transferred from your bank as well. Compared to these options, a cash value policy can be a relatively expensive way to feed your piggy bank.

It can also serve as a very conservative way to add to your security and growth baskets. Insurance companies do invest part of your premium into conservative investments such as real estate and bonds.

These investments have provided a regular dividend which builds up in the cash value account of the policy. This cash value is yours and can be accessed before you die or it can be used to pay the insurance premiums on the policy after several years down the road.

Disability Insurance

Disability insurance, often called disability income insurance, insures the beneficiary's earned income against the risk that disability will make working (and therefore earning) impossible. It includes paid sick leave, short-term disability benefits, and long-term disability benefits.

In general, premiums are higher for policies that provided more monthly benefit, pay the benefit for a longer period of time, and start payments for benefits more quickly following a disability. Premiums also tend to be higher for policies that define disability in broader terms, meaning the policy would pay benefits in a wider variety of circumstances.

Generally, there are three major types of individual long-term-disability-policies:

(1) Non-cancelable policy: your premiums are fixed over the term of the policy. The insurer cannot jack up the rates, decrease your benefits, cancel or refuse to renew the policy.

(2) Guaranteed renewable policy: your premiums can be raised so long as the change affects an entire category of occupations, policyholders,   etc.

(3) Conditionally renewable policies: your premiums can go up and your coverage canceled in the event any conditions stated in the policy are triggered.

For the purposes of our financial wellness it is enough to be familiar with what disability insurance is and that it is available. There is a premium that must be paid for the insurance so many people opt out and take their chances that they will never need it.

My recommendation is that it depends on the type of work that you do. If you are susceptible to personal injury on the job, than it might be a good idea to have.

Here in the United States, the Social Security System offers disability insurance as well. The wait time is generally longer to get benefits (income) and more stringent requirements must be met. But it is income if you meet the requirements set up by the government.

Bank Account Types

Money Market Accounts

The best place to put the money that you are saving for your six months of living expenses is in a money market account. These can be set up easily at your local bank. The reason that I like this product more than a bank savings account is that it pays more interest on your money.

It's easy to move funds between local bank checking account and the money market account. We just need to plan ahead a little when transferring money between accounts because depending on the amount, it can take a few days to show up. However, the difference in the amount of interest we earn is well worth the effort of setting up a money market account.

If you need to access those funds to replenish your checking account, then money can easily move without having to leave home or office. One of the nice benefits of today's technology is that funds can be accessed online from the comfort of home any time of day. It is certainly more convenient rather than going to the bank and waiting in line.

Checking Accounts

Checking accounts are a good place to keep the money to pay ongoing and reoccurring monthly expenses. These include mortgage payment, utilities, phone, and credit card bills (you always want to pay off your credit card bill each month). This is also where we want to have our check writing coming from. Keep things simple by having one account to write checks from.

Make sure to balance the checking account every month. Do yourself a big favor by getting into the habit of doing this within a few days of getting the bank statement.

Or, get the statement online. The bank can send an email alerting you when the statement is available.

Print the statement and use it to balance the checking account. It's simple and fun to do because it only takes a few minutes. Maybe you can tell that being organized is important to financial wellness?

Start using financial software if you haven't already. It's great for your household bookkeeping because it simplifies it.

It's a good way to keep track of the checking account and makes balancing the account much easier. It's a great for keeping track of investments and other assets as well.

Having all accounts in one place makes it very easy to see your net worth, what investments you have, and the different types of accounts such as Roth IRAs and traditional IRAs. You can update the value whenever you want and generate reports to know the history of the different financial accounts.

Keeping track of investments is definitely an integral part of the Financial Wellness process because financial information is at your fingertips. This all leads down that road called financial peace of mind which is crucial to your cause.

After balancing the bank statement, it is a good idea to keep it with the check receipts and other banking receipts for the month in a safe place. This can be a large envelope to keep in a desk drawer or filing cabinet. The point is to do this every month so that you have the last twelve months of statements saved and can refer to if ever needed.

Sometimes things come up that require you to go back and check the figures on a canceled check to help balance a statement. It's nice to be able to go back in the records and find the missing check or receipt for the given month. This is why it's a good idea to file away each month's statement with the receipts for that month.

To keep files from stacking up over time, after the statements are more than a year old, through them away. Better yet, shred them so there is no chance of identity theft.

There are ways to use technology to simplify further your personal finances. NeatReceipts is one that uses a scanner to capture receipts, business cards, and other information while the software automatically organizes key information on your computer.

Use online bill pay and automatic withdrawal for many of your monthly payments such as for the phone bill, utilities, and credit cards. Managing finances has never been easier!

Dual or Single Checking Accounts?

For couples, the question of whether it is better to have dual or single checking accounts has come up and is an important consideration. Finances are often complicated by previous marriages, child support or alimony, student loans, existing mortgages or credit card debt, and other issues such as a sense of autonomy and financial independence.

I know that for my wife and I when we first got married we set up a joint account and we each had our own checkbook. It didn't take long to figure out that this was not a good idea because we each kept forgetting to enter checks that we had written and trying to balance the statement at the end of the month was a real hassle. We switched to having one checkbook and designated one person to balance it.

We could both write checks and another big improvement was having carbon copies. This gave us a hard copy of all the checks we had written in case we forgot to account for the check in our register.

Then when we started using computer software to keep track of our checking account, these carbon copies became indispensable. I used these carbon copies to enter in the checks that we had written.

I could do this once a week, or whenever I wanted. This system of having one person manage the checking account has worked well for managing our household spending needs.

One Joint Account

This is what I recommend using because it's worked well for my family. If you're both comfortable with this approach, it's certainly the easiest to maintain.

It works best when one person is the main one managing the account. Pick the one that enjoys it the most to be the person that is in charge of the account. You can also switch back and forth to take turns if you want.

The One-Two Method (One Joint Account Plus Two Separate Accounts)

Many couples today set up a joint checking account while retaining their separate checking accounts. They each pay an agreed upon amount into the joint checking account each month and use this account to pay the household bills. One of the big advantages to this method is that each person retains his or her own autonomy and financial independence and that helps avoid the use of money as power in the relationship.

If the One-Two method is used, come up with a method of determining how much each of you will contribute to the joint checking account. To do this:

1. If you both earn roughly the same amount, it makes sense to each contribute the same dollar amount to the joint account. If one of you earns substantially more than the other, it's fair to contribute on a percentage basis.
2. Set up a joint checking account that each of you contributes to for the shared household expenses.
3. Continue to pay your own pre-existing credit card debt, student loans, and other financial obligations from your personal checking accounts.

Neither of these methods is right or wrong. Resentment over money can fester and eventually poison a relationship if it's not addressed in a way that satisfies each partner, so what's right is what works for you as a couple. It's important to long-term relationships that each of you feels good about how the money works in the relationship.

Example: You earn $60,000 per year. Your spouse earns $40,000 per year, for a total of $100,000 joint income.

Determine the contribution by performing the following calculations:

1. Add your annual income to your spouse's annual income.
2. Divide one salary by the total combined salaries to get a percentage. $60,000 / $100,000 = .6 or 60%
3. Multiply this percentage times the dollar amount you need in the joint account monthly to pay your shared bills. This is one earning spouses' monthly contribution. .6 x $3,000 = $1,800
4. Subtract this amount from the dollar amount needed in the account monthly. This is the other earning spouse's contribution. $3,000 - $1,800 = $1,200.

This is a fair way to allocate the two different incomes into one checking account to pay for reoccurring monthly expenses and other annual household expenses that come from living together in a home and possibly raising a family.

Credit Cards

Credit cards are a great tool at our disposal as a convenience. They make paying for things so much faster and easier than paying with cash or with a check. They are also easy to carry around in purse or wallet.

Our culture requires that we have one to pay for certain things such as rental cars or to reserve a room at a hotel. They also serve well as a quick and easy way to build a good credit rating needed when getting a home or a car loan.

My favorite amenity of having a credit card is all the airline miles I rack up by using it. I've accumulated hundreds of thousands of miles over the years and use them to pay for the more expensive flights that I take when I go with my family on vacation.

I have a rule of thumb, use the miles when an airline ticket would cost me more than $400. I've used miles on many occasions to fly overseas when tickets would normally cost me over $600. Credit cards are good to use and help in your personal financial wellness plan.

Credit cards work like this: when you buy something, you are creating a debt that needs to be paid in the future. In other words, you're getting an instant loan from the bank that issued the card.

You haven't paid for what was charged on the card, you've borrowed the money from the bank and the bank paid it. The bank therefore adds up all these little "loans" and sends an itemized statement at the end of the month with a total.

Let me give you a huge secret to achieving Financial Wellness at this time. This is very important and many people have not learned this and have gotten themselves in a huge amount of trouble.

PAY OFF YOUR CREDIT CARD STATEMENT IN FULL EVERY MONTH!

Even if you have to take money out of your savings/money market account to do so, you must commit to paying back your credit card "loans" each month.

The reason this is so important is that these banks charge a very high interest rate on these mini-loans if they aren't paid back at the end of the month.

However, if you pay back these loans, there is no interest at all. They are basically giving mini-loans all through the month, and they don't charge any interest as long as they're paid back when they send the bill.

If not paid back, they hit you with very high interest rates. These rates are very commonly over 20% per year. Imagine getting a home or car loan and having to pay 20% or more per year in interest. That is exactly what you're doing when you don't pay the credit card bill in full every month.

You are telling the bank to hit you with that high interest rate, and the banks love it. That is one reason why they created the credit card industry in the first place. This is a huge profit center for banks. This is good for the banks, but not good for you.

Large retail chain stores are the same way. The credit card that they issue with their store name on the card, this is a huge profit center for them as well. They know that many of their customers will not pay off the bill when it comes in the mail, and they will get to charge 20% or more per year in interest on the "loan" they just gave.

The best advice I can give regarding these retail store credit cards is just say, "No!" Having said that however, the only time we should accept them is if we are buying a particularly high-dollar item, and they're offering a discount if we get one of their credit cards. There are three requirements that have to be met before accepting this offer.

- The purchase has to be sufficiently large so that the discount we get is going to be worth the effort.

- We have to pay off the bill in full, no exceptions, when it comes in the mail.

- When the actual card comes in the mail, you will have to call the customer service number on the card and CANCEL the card immediately.

Debit Cards

Debit cards are very different than credit cards in that when we use them to buy something, the money actually does come out of our bank account right away. In other words, we aren't taking out a loan from the bank like we are with a credit card. This can be a very good thing for those of you that don't trust yourselves to pay off your credit card bills at the end of each month.

Since debit cards are not buying things by taking out a mini-loan, this means that we will not be building a credit rating because we aren't "buying on credit".

Having a good credit rating is important though. Credit cards, if used properly, are an easy and quick way to do that. Making your mortgage payment or apartment rent on time every month, as well as your other monthly bills, also contribute to your credit rating.

Debit cards can even earn airline miles at some banks. It's also easy to get cash when using a debit card because many retailers can give cash from the card at check-out.

Credit Scores

Part of maintaining our financial wellness is making sure that we have a good credit rating and it really isn't that hard to do. The reason we want to keep a good credit rating, or high credit rating, is that it will make our financial life easier.

For example, a high credit score helps us in being charged lower interest rates for loans, being approved for credit cards, home, student, and car loans. Some employers check the credit score of their potential job candidates, so a good credit score could aid us in getting the job we want. Here are some simple steps that will help us all keep a good credit rating:

- *Start out with just one credit card,* and keep the habit of having only one or two credit cards. Many first-time credit card users accumulate a collection of credit cards within their first few years of using credit. Don't do this. The more credit you have, the more you'll end up using.

- *We don't want to max out any of our credit cards* or even get close. Keeping our credit use to less than 30% of your credit limits (10% is better) will help us get the best possible credit scores. Lenders know that borrowers who max out their cards often have difficulty repaying what they've borrowed.

- *Pay off credit card bills and other bills on time*. There is no substitute for this habit. If we do this we'll have no problem maintaining a high credit score.

Here's a quick reference to what defines a good credit score versus a bad credit score according to the credit rating agencies and some banking institutions.

- *An excellent credit rating is anything above 750*. The rating chart goes from 350 up to 850 points as the highest possible score.

- *A good credit rating is at least a 720*. If your score is 720, there's really no need to try and raise it because lenders tend to lump people in the same category as those with a score of say 800 or 820."

- *The national average is around 725 points*.

- *A score of 620 or lower is considered a low credit score and risky for lenders*. Borrowers will have to pay higher interest rates and will have a harder time getting credit.

- *Anything below 550 is considered not a good credit rating*.

One of the downsides of having a good credit score is that lenders will target you as a great possible new customer, and they will send you lots of credit card and home equity loan offers in the mail. This is mostly junk mail, and you should treat it as such. It goes directly into the recycle bin.

As mentioned earlier, a good credit score has many more benefits than the downside of getting lots of credit card offers in the mail to be thrown into the trash. The following is a possible example of the benefit of a good credit score on getting a mortgage on a home:

Take a typical couple who is considering buying their first home: Let's say they want a thirty-year mortgage loan and their FICO credit scores are **720**. They could qualify for a mortgage with a low 5.5 percent interest rate*.

But if their scores are **580**, they probably would pay 8.5 percent* or more -- that's at least three full percentage points more in interest.

On a $100,000 mortgage loan, that three point difference will cost them $3,000 dollars a year, adding up to $90,000 dollars more over the loan's 30-year lifetime. $90,000 is a lot of money for having a low credit score.

*An approximation of what interest rates are in 2010 for a 30-year mortgage.

The Skinny on Debt

Three Steps to Debt Management:

1. Don't have any debt.
2. If you have debt, pay it off as soon as you can even if you have to get a second job.
3. Refer back to #1 and #2.

Paying off your personal debt is one of the best ways to save money. The reason is that the interest rate paid on certain kinds of debt can be very high, higher probably than any return on investments. In other words, you rob your savings accounts (your future dollars) to pay the lenders that you're borrowing from.

The idea is to pay off the highest cost debt first and keep paying off other debts until left only with debt that has a lower cost than the return on the investments. It is a good idea to take into account the true cost of debt at this juncture:

Mortgage Debt

This debt here in the U.S. is special because the IRS allows us to deduct the interest we pay each year on our home loan from our federal income tax. So the true cost of the debt is reduced by the amount of taxes we save each year which can take a 5% interest rate to a tax equivalent 4% as an example (using a 20% income tax bracket).

All Debt is Not Bad Debt

There is such a thing as good debt! This takes the form of borrowing money to build something that will have a higher value or will create a higher value than the cost of the debt.

Examples are:

☆ Borrowing to buy a business

☆ For investment property

☆ To purchase and install equipment in a factory or purchase raw materials for production

☆ To buy inventory for resale

☆ Short-term financing of employee payroll until an invoice is paid

```
┌─────────────────────────────────────┐
│                                       │
│       **Debt Reduction Killers:**     │
│                                       │
│       Things that will cost a lot of  │
│       money in the long run!          │
│                                       │
│            1.  Convenience            │
│            2.  Indulgence             │
│            3.  Appearance             │
│                                       │
└─────────────────────────────────────┘
```

Bad Debt

Bad debt is money borrowed for expenses that are not necessary. These have gotten out of hand because credit was so easily obtained and interest rates were so low that the temptation to borrow was too great to resist.

An example of bad debt would be to borrow money to go on a vacation. The better approach would be to save the money ahead of time and then go on the vacation.

The Rule of Thumb for Knowing if it is Bad Debt

Are you able to pay off the debt in full at the end of each month? If not, then you should ask yourself this question: Is this debt going to continue to increase if I don't change my spending habits now?

Why save money?

In order to be successful at adopting and keeping up with the habit of saving money, have a reason to do so. There are just too many temptations to spend money on things that do not have a lasting effect on our lives. Here are a few practical reasons saving money is a good thing:

1. Have a cushion for unexpected expenses that creep up on us. Car expenses, house expenses, clothing, entertainment with friends or family, etc.

2. If you can't save you can't invest and have money work for you! You get no compounding of interest advantage which is huge regarding long-term investment success.

3. Peace of mind! "I know from the research conducted on my book on financial happiness that people who manage to put away at least 5% of their earnings every month feel significantly better than those who don't." Jean Chatzky, "The Difference".

4. Power! If you have money in the bank you have the power to make decisions instead of others making decisions for you. If your industry changes and you want to change careers, you can! If you want to move to another part of the country for a better lifestyle, you can! If you want a larger home because your family is growing, you can! If you need another car because one of the kids is driving now, buy one!

To summarize the chapter on building our security basket, here is a list of the main themes that should take the mystery out of beginning our long-term Financial Wellness.

1. Spend less than you make and invest the difference, whatever that may be per month.

2. Use a monthly budget to compare your necessary living expenses to your income.

3. Pay yourselves first! To give you an idea of what this amount should be, make your goal 10% of what you earn as a starting point. You can go up to 15% or 20%+ as well, depending on personal circumstances. Subtract your total expenses from your total income per month. This is the amount to save per month. Put this amount aside on the first day of each month before doing anything else. One way to do this is set up an automatic withdraw from your checking account into a money market account. Hold it here until you've accumulated enough to invest.

4. Spend what is left over after you've covered the investment percentage and necessary living expense amounts. Life is also about laughing, loving and living, so set some money aside for enjoying your lives. Even if the amount is small, there are many things that you can do that require little, if any, money.

5. Here are some examples of things we can do that cost little or no money:
    - go to the movies
    - day trips to a museum

- go to the park for a picnic lunch
- take a walk
- go downtown for a stroll
- ride your bike
- get together with friends or family
- play sports
- jog
- read a book
- learn a new skill
- practice playing a musical instrument
- volunteer

Building a security basket is not as bad as some people might think. It doesn't matter if you're 18 or 80, the security basket is the foundation of Financial Wellness. Like building a house, the foundation takes a little while to come together, but it's worth every bit of time and money that was put in to make it sound.

The better the foundation is the bigger and taller the growth and preservation baskets will be and ultimately the better the overall finances. The return on investment in the security basket will be many times over what you put into it, and it's never too late to start.

∞

Chapter 7

Basket #2 – Growth

Once the security basket begins to over flow with extra money that you don't need for living expenses, begin to move the surplus over into the growth basket. What you'll find in this basket predominantly are investments for a future need or desired lifestyle and also for funding a retirement.

Money grows through allocating cash consistently to this basket over time, proper asset diversification, compounding of interest and long-term sound investment strategies. Tools in the basket include 401Ks/457(b)s and Individual Retirement Accounts (IRAs), individual company stocks, mutual funds, ETFs, options, real estate, and alternative investments.

There is no shortage of ideas and products that can be used to grow assets. The main thing here to keep in mind is to have a long term approach and to stay the course.

With patience and persistence, the growth will come over time. You will want to study up on the different investment techniques but keep in mind that historically the more simple strategies do fine for most people.

For the more sophisticated investor with more wealth to manage, there are usually more opportunities to participate in more complicated but possibly higher return investment ideas.

Typically these investments have the ability to return a better than average yield for the investor.

It is very important to investors at this growth basket level to ensure that assets are well-managed to minimize risk while taking advantage of any growth prospects. The last thing you want to do is lose money over a long period of time instead of making money. Unfortunately, this can happen if you take on too much risk with a large portion of the investments.

Another possibility during investing in this growth basket is that the markets can go down in value as well. This goes for the real estate market as well as the stock market and holds true especially with more speculative investments. You must always be willing to ride out the inevitable down-times in the investments. This is why it is best to have a long term approach in this basket.

Short Investment Horizon?

If your approach to investing is not so long term, say ten years or less, then it's best to mix up your growth investments with a significant portion going to the capital preservation basket. The mix will keep the portfolio exposed to the growth side of the markets but will not overexpose you in case things do not go as planned.

You still want to be exposed to the growth side of the markets to some extent to keep up with inflation that has been about 3% per year on average in our country for many years now. So, keep up with inflation at the very least. This can be accomplished with several investment products in the market.

For example, corporate bonds traditionally have returned approximately 5% to 6% per year. On the other hand, stocks have traditionally returned about 9% to 11% per year.

Therefore, a mix of stocks and bonds should be able to keep up with inflation if the historical rates and returns are considered. Of course, there are always exceptions, and there could be a trend in both rates of inflation and rates of return that are not following the average. In fact, that is all they are, averages, and the reality is that the actual rates and returns for any given year can be quite different on the upside as well as on the downside.

Why am telling you all this? It's important for the growth investor to realize that the stock market does not always behave rationally or follow along the general sentiment of the investing public. There have been times when the market goes in quite the opposite direction from what the majority of people thought.

This can mean that the market could go up when the general feeling is that it will go down and vice versa. This is why having a least a ten-year investment outlook for investments in this growth basket is a way for us to not worry too much about the month to month and year to year behavior of the market that can be somewhat erratic at times.

What to Expect When ~~Expecting~~ Investing!

I'm having a little fun with this analogy of "expecting" as in giving birth to a baby. My wife and I read the pregnancy guide "What To Expect When You Are Expecting" by Heidi Murkoff and Sharon Mazel, 1984.

It is known as the bible for pregnant mothers, and I know it helped us in coping with our first pregnancy. If we think about it, there are some very similar characteristics between having and raising a child and building a financial growth basket.

They both can be a very exciting and important part of our lives. They both need nurturing from the very beginning and eventually, after they grow and mature, they take on a life of their own. They can become our life's pride and joy as we forget about the many bumps and struggles along the way as they were growing up.

Okay, maybe I've taken it a little bit too far here with the analogy, but I think you get the picture. As wonderful as children are, it doesn't mean that everything goes perfectly as planned all the time.

As a parent, I know that my range of emotions has been expanded because of my children. My emotions have gone up to new highs and sometimes fallen to new lows and everywhere in between.

Being an investor in the growth basket can take on some very similar emotional attributes. A good example of this emotional roller coaster is the last ten years when the stock market has been a very volatile. Investors have been experiencing and dealing with a variety of emotions during this time, and I believe we could still have another six to eight years of similar volatility.

The graph below shows the emotional rollercoaster that investors can go through in a volatile market. A friend of mine who is a member of the clergy said that this graph shows the same emotional points that someone feels when they experience the different stages of grief over the loss of a loved one. These feelings are real and very heart-felt.

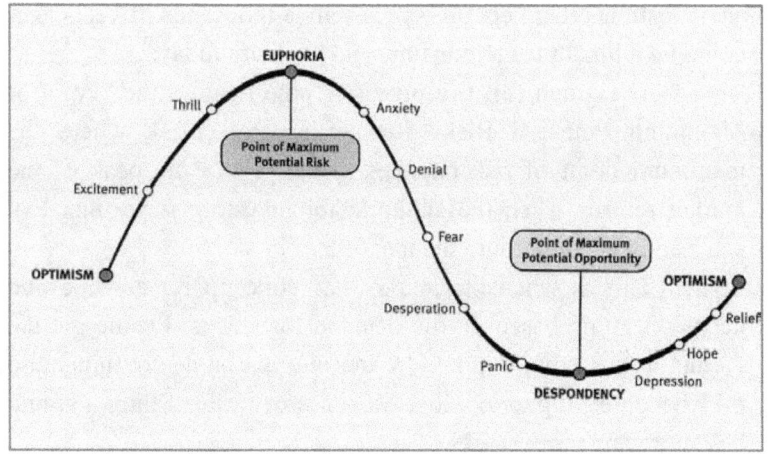

These emotions are a reason the mutual fund industry does so well. Fund managers feed off the public's inability to handle the emotions money provokes.

Most people can't deal with it (emotions) so they hand their money over to a fund manager. What's ironic is that fund managers suffer from the same problem, and this is a primary reason most active money managers underperform the stock market.

Our emotions have been hard-wired in us as best as we can explain it going back thousands of years. We adopted **either** a flight or fight emotional makeup depending on what was going on around us at the time.

A simple explanation of how we developed our emotional instinct is if we felt confident and optimistic in our abilities to survive the situation at hand, we stood and fought. On the other hand, if we were feeling overwhelmed, we became fearful, panicked, and ran away.

Both of these emotions helped us survive and eventually flourish in the jungles, savannahs and mountains that our ancestors lived in. Fast-forward to our digital world where the same instincts that kept our species alive thousands of years ago, could be a hindrance to our financial wellness today.

The graph **(on the previous page)** shows the "Point of Maximum Potential Risk" for an investor. Look where the maximum point of risk happens to be! It's at the peak of the market returns when the euphoria for investing is so high that everybody is getting into the market.

This is when the market has gone up for a while and keeps on going based on the demand for stocks. People get the feeling at this point that they're missing out on a sure thing, and they become "euphoric", lose all sense of rational thinking, and buy more and more stocks.

During this time, we hear things like, "our neighbor bought 'such and such' stock, and it has gone up 30% over the last two months." After we hear this kind of thing from several different people, we start to question whether we're putting enough into the market, and we may buy the same investments that we've been hearing about.

This unfortunately is precisely the wrong time to be buying. But, we have a very hard time understanding that because of our innate and habitual emotional reaction to the excitement and thrill of winning and not being left out.

On the contrary, this is actually the best time to be selling. Remember the saying, "buy low and sell high?" When everybody else is buying and driving up the prices, that is when the market is too high and, as the graph shows, is the best time to sell.

This is extremely hard to do, and that's why market timing is a difficult strategy to implement. It's very hard to know when the top is and then to actually pull the trigger because nobody really knows for sure.

The same applies to the other end of the spectrum on the graph marked "Point of Maximum Potential Opportunity." After the market has gone down to such an extent that investors have passed through the stages of fear, desperation, panic, and despondency, it can be very difficult to buy back into the market. But, as we can see from the graph, that's the best time to buy because the market has hit its low point and is going back up again.

Benjamin Graham, who is considered the Father of Value Investing and who was an early mentor to Warren Buffet, said that, "The investor's chief problem, and even his worst enemy, is likely to be himself." We really just want to be aware of the emotions that can come in this growth basket stage.

If we're aware of this element of investing, then we can guard against it by having someone help us make decisions when we are feeling out of sorts. Investment strategies that bypass emotions work well here. After all, we are after financial wellness in our lives, not financial stress.

How to Succeed in the Growth Basket

Different times call for different strategies when investing in the "growth" basket. We obviously want our hard-earned assets to grow in this stage, in fact, we are counting on it. After all, this is where our "preservation" basket money is going to come from which we will talk about later. How do we succeed in the growth basket?

First of all, make sure that the time horizon is long enough, five years at the minimum. This is because the swings in the growth market can be such that if you need the money back before five years, you may have less than you started with. This is a risk that every investor takes, and it's called market risk. This is true whether you're talking about the stock market or the real estate market.

Second, make sure that you're following a system that's working. During the 80s and 90s, the strategy that worked was buy and hold, which for many of us meant that we bought a mutual fund that was doing well and held it as we added more to it over time.

However, over the last decade, that same system hasn't worked at all. Now there is a new system that works. It involves moving into sectors that are building strength and moving out of sectors that are losing strength.

This is not to be confused with day-trading or market-timing. It is more trend analysis-based investing and compares the relative strength of certain sectors against others. It also includes the ability to go into cash in a significant way which is something the buy-and-hold strategy does not allow.

Since no strategy works all the time, every time, and forever, being flexible and open to new investment ideas is important to maintain growth over the long-term. What works now may not work a few years from now, or even a few months from now.

Having a source of information that you can trust and having a professional advisor that's able to put your interest above theirs is crucial in this "growth" basket environment. Having worked in a corporate environment, I can tell you, unfortunately, investment firms are more interested in *their* bottom line than in yours.

Having enough time ahead of you, finding a system that works, and being flexible enough to make changes, should do the job of growing money in this "growth" basket. After all, the goal of this basket is to grow assets to feed the next basket, the basket of preserving wealth.

> *Key to wealth accumulation over time is not about how much money we make when we are right, it is more about how much money we keep ourselves from losing when we are wrong that will determine our wealth over time.*

Conservative or Aggressive Growth?

Growth investing can be broken down into two approaches: a conservative growth strategy or an aggressive growth strategy. People in general will think they fall into the aggressive growth side because they want their assets to grow as quickly as possible. It seems to make sense, that if given the choice, we'd rather have growth be fast.

That would be true, however, in investing there is no free lunch. If you want aggressive growth you'll most likely encounter more volatility in the value of assets over the course of the investment time frame. You'll have to put up with the value going down possibly 30% and then rebounding at some point, hopefully!

Ask yourself if you'd be comfortable with that drop of 30% and all the while not being certain when or if it will bounce back. Many people are not willing to take that kind of possible scenario with all their money.

A person's investment horizon also is an important consideration in determining whether conservative or aggressive growth is the right one for them. If the funds will not be needed for many years, then possibly an aggressive approach is appropriate. On the other hand, if the number of years that the money will be left in the investment before it's needed is not very long, maybe the more conservative strategy is better suited.

Another determinant that should be used to qualify someone as a conservative or aggressive growth candidate is the percentage of their estate or the amount of money available for investing compared to their overall net worth. Only a certain amount of a person's estate should be used for growth investing because it's the more risky part of their investments.

Don't put at risk all of the money. An intelligent amount should be set aside for growth investing especially if an aggressive growth strategy is the one chosen by the investor.

It's important to approach growth investing with some thought and consideration regarding the above mentioned conditions. Growth investing is an extremely important basket in financial wellness because it is where money earns the maximum return on investment. Return is an important part of growth investing, however careful contemplation must be followed here.

The selection between conservative and aggressive is also a personality issue. Some investors like to play it safe and let someone else take on the emotional up and down investment rides.

Others want to feel like they're getting as much out of the market as possible and don't want to leave any money on the table. Most people fall in the middle somewhere. A big part of deciding what approach is more appropriate depends on which one is more like you.

Pitfalls to Growth Investing

I know that over the last ten years growth investing has been a non-event for most investors. Therefore, there's a lot of pessimism and skepticism of the stock market and for good reason.

Many people missed the roaring 80s and 90s and started investing in the late nineties. Then the dot com bubble burst followed by 9/11.

The stock market started looking good again from 2003 to 2007 and then came 2008 with the great financial crisis. By the end of 2009, the market had recovered from the lows earlier in the year but, by then, the damage had been done. A decade-long overall loss to patient buy-and-hold investors resulted.

Many were left scratching their head and wondered what happened. Buy-and-hold was the way they were taught to invest for the long term. The investing experts advised that the inevitable ups and downs would come along, but if we just held on long enough, we'd all be saved by hanging in there over time.

Well the result for the ten years between the year 2000 and 2009 was a negative 3%, and it doesn't look much better for the next six to eight years either.

The long-term market cycles graph **on the next page** shows a sixteen-to-eighteen-year cycle that alternates from a consolidation period to a growth period and back again. These growth and consolidation cycles actually go back to the late 1800s when the financial industry started tracking the stock market.

After the crash of 1929, a consolidation period lasted through the depression era and did not turn into a growth cycle until after WWII. The post WWII era ushered in the next growth cycle until roughly 1966, when the next consolidation cycle began.

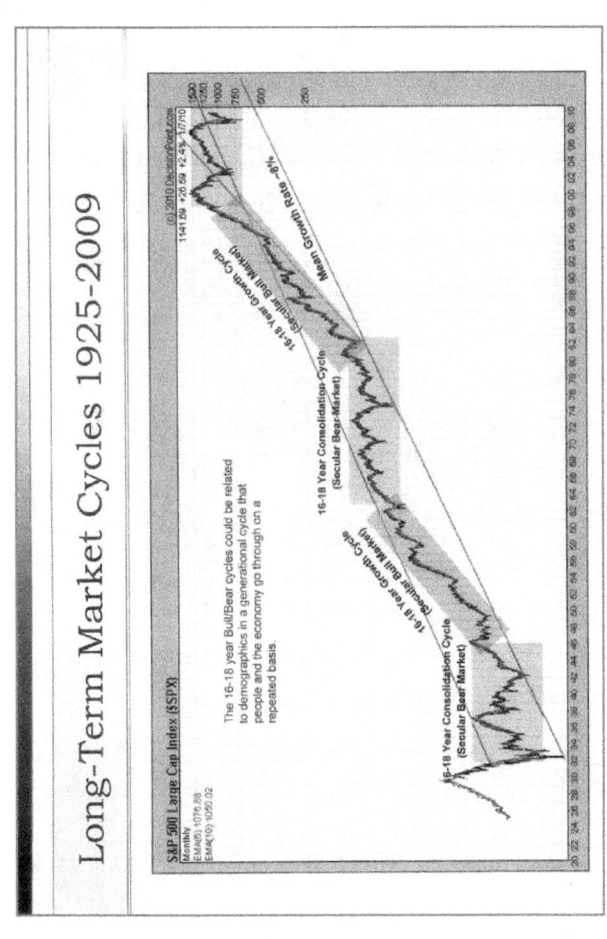

Long-Term Market Cycles 1925-2009

69

Consolidation Market: 1966 - 1982

Prior to the last great bull market of the 80s and 90s, the market was in a long term consolidation period that lasted from 1966 to 1982. During this time, the market essentially went sideways for sixteen years.

The Dow hit a high of about 1000 in 1966, and a low in the 800s in 1982. If investors followed brokers' advice to "hold for the long term" they would have been greatly disappointed. Sixteen years is a long time to receive nothing in return.

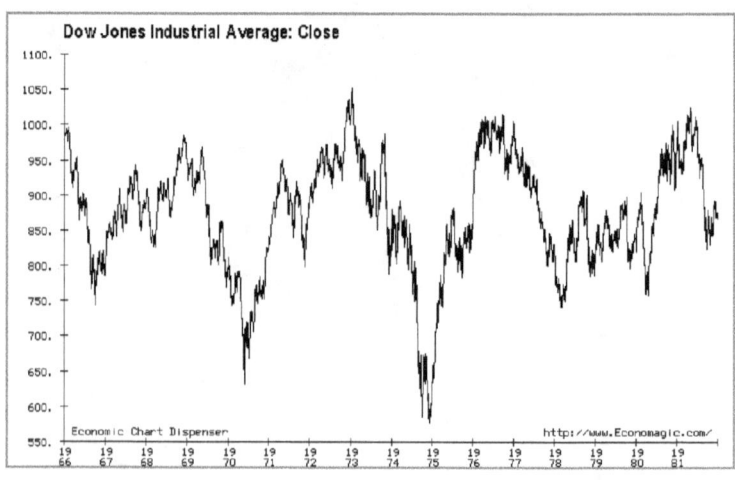

The chart of the Dow above from 1966 to 1982 is a classic example of what a consolidation market looks like. There were strong bull and bear markets within this time period that caused the market to essentially remain flat for sixteen years. However, these bull and bear markets could be traded and some investors did just that.

If a time machine existed that could jump forward eight years, this is how a chart of the stock market might look for the years between 2000 and 2016. If that's true, investors will need to do their homework, seeking sectors that present great opportunities to make any money over the next six to eight years.

Going Solo

Investors in this growth basket can rely on their own study and analysis in deciding what to invest in. However, after investing for twenty years, I need to issue a warning here.

The two most common biases that get investors in trouble are over-optimism and over-confidence. Over-confidence refers to a situation whereby people are surprised more often than they expect to be. Effectively people are generally much too sure about their ability to predict.

Studies reveal the worst performers are generally the most over-confident. They argue that such individuals suffer a double curse of being unskilled and unaware of it. The problem is that the skills needed to produce correct responses are virtually identical to those needed to self-evaluate the potential accuracy of responses, hence the problem.

This is irony in action. Knowledge drives over-confidence, so people that actually know something about a topic are more prone to think they can forecast, and they probably even sound more believable.

This may be one of the few instances in which ignorance is bliss. If we have the "beginner's mind" and don't make any assumptions about what might happen, we're going to be better off than if we are knowledgeable and try to guess.

Systematic trend-following eliminates the need to forecast (although apparently not the desire, since clients constantly ask us what we think is going to happen). At JB Wealth Management, we use relative strength to drive our trend-following; it's able to pick out the strongest trends, and those are the trends we are interested in following.

We stay with an asset as long as it remains strong. When it weakens, we kick it out of the portfolio and replace it with something stronger. This kind of casting-out method allows the portfolio to adapt to the market environment, as it's constantly refreshed with new, strong assets.

Advantages in the Growth Basket

The Power of Compounding

The Rule of 72: How many years will it take for my money to double at a given compounding interest rate?

% interest	Years to double
2%	36
3%	24
4%	18
5%	14
6%	12
7%	10
8%	9
10%	7
12%	6
14%	5
16%	4.5
18%	4
20%	3.6

One of the best examples I've heard about what the power of compounding can do is depicted in the following real life story.

In 1626, Manhattan Island was bought from the Manhattan Indians by Peter Minuit, Governor of the West India Company. He paid $24 dollars worth of beads, cloth, and trinkets to the tribe. If that same $24 had been invested back then by the Indians in a money market equivalent investment (they didn't have these back then) its value would be enough today to buy back the whole island of Manhattan in its present state!

Now that's the power of compounding over time. In less than 400 years, a $24 dollar investment could have grown to trillions of dollars. What is equally interesting is that a mere $24 bought the island of Manhattan less than 400 years ago. Sounds like Peter Minuit knew a good deal when he saw one.

No one would argue now that investing in the New World back then would turn out to be a very good investment over time. America was definitely a growth investment because it has grown by leaps and bounds over the last 400 years although there have been many fits and starts along the way.

Similarly, the U.S. stock market over the last 100+ years has definitely been a growth story as well but not without its own ups and downs. Here are some interesting stats and growth rates for the Dow Jones Industrial Average:

- The yearly return from 1900 (end-of-year 1899) through 2009 was approximately 9.4% (4.7% price appreciation, plus approx 4.7% in dividends)

- The return from 1929 (End-of-year 1928 -- i.e., before the crash) thru 2009 was 8.8% (4.5%, plus 4.3%)

- From end-of-year 1932 (i.e., after the crash) - 2009: 11.1% (6.9%, plus 4.2%)

- For the last twenty-five years, the annual return was 11.9% (9.0%, plus 2.9%)
- For the last 20 years, 9.4% (6.9%, plus 2.5%)

- For the last 10 years, 1.3% (-1.0%, plus 2.3%)

- For the last 5 years, 1.9% (-0.7%, plus 2.6%)

- For 2009 the stock market (Dow/DJIA) return was 22.0% (18.8% plus 3.2%)

Even though the last ten years has seen a very low growth rate in the Dow of only 1.3%, this is not the only time that has happened. The growth rate in the decade of the 1970s was only 5% for the whole ten years. Here are some interesting facts about ten year investing periods from the past:

The Best and Worst Ten-Year Returns in Dow Jones History (since 1900)

In hindsight, when would have been the best and worst years to buy?

The _best_ ten-year periods to own stocks were the years beginning in:

- 1918: the return was about 19.5% per year for the next ten years.

- 1948 & 49: 18.5% annual return.

- 1987 & 88: about 18.5% annual return.

The _worst_ ten-year period to buy were:

- 1922: the return was 0.4% per year for the next ten years.

- 1928: -1.3% annual return (loss), because you would have had the great misfortune of buying just before the 1929-1932 stock market crash.

- 1964: annual return of 0.3% for the next ten years.

It is interesting to note that from the list of the best ten-year periods to buy stocks are the years after a huge and global event came to an end. In 1918, it was the end of the WWI. 1948 was three years after the end of WWII.

1988 was right before the peaceful end of the Soviet Union and the Cold War between the U.S. and Russia. It was right before the Berlin Wall crumbled and ushered in a sense of change, promise, and opportunity for the whole world.

It makes me wonder what big global event is coming in the near future that, when it ends, may usher in another best ten-year period to buy domestic stocks. Will the end of some current event usher in a global resurgence of investment and growth? Will it have similar favorable repercussions with a change from turmoil to peace?

What is going on right now is the emergence of economies around the world that are not as developed and industrialized as is the U.S. and other first world countries. With access to capital and know-how and the leveling of the information playing field, countries that have not participated in the growth of the last several decades will, hopefully, now benefit.

These emerging economies such as China, Brazil, Russia, India, Vietnam, Columbia, and Egypt just to name a few in addition to other Middle Eastern, Asian, African, and Latin American countries will no doubt be success stories to come. If they can keep their countries and governments stable along with good economic policies, the flow of capital will go wherever it is needed to reap the inevitable returns.

That has been the growth story of the U.S and Western Europe. These were stable countries with good economic policies and prospects and the flow of capital went there to fuel their success over the last 100 to 200 years.

This will be the same story going forward. Growth investors are always looking at countries that have the best prospects for growth, and they take all the above into consideration. At the end of the day, and in today's financial markets where money can be given and taken away immediately through our digital networks, the countries that get the funding from investors are the ones that offer the best prospects for sustainable growth.

Regarding the worst ten-year period to buy stocks in the U.S, they can be explained as well. The 1920s had the worst fall in the history of the stock market in 1929, and it did not get much better during the 1930s. Not until the end of WWII did the stock market become a great investment again for about the next sixteen years until 1964.

The ten-year period following 1964 in the U.S. had many social upheavals and transitions. President Kennedy had been assassinated and many say that is when the U.S. lost its innocence. The Vietnam War took a very heavy toll on our confidence. During this time our nation paid a high price in financing a war, human life, and a sense of loss in direction.

The Civil Rights Movement, the sexual revolution, and the hippie era were huge social and cultural transitions for our country. Fortunately, there were many innovations during that time that laid the ground work for the technological breakthroughs that helped lay the foundation for the next growth period of the 1980s and 1990s.

In the 1990s, the growth engine was pretty much technology companies and the advancement of the information highway of the Internet. In the first years of the 2000s, housing and consumer spending was the fuel of the economy.

The big question on investor's minds now is what is the next big thing that will drive the growth in the stock market? Some ideas that could come to be the next engines of growth here in the U.S are:

Health Care

With our many research universities around the country, we may be building up to reap the benefits of some big breakthroughs in medical technology and health care. People are certainly interested in living longer and more active lifestyles, and the demand for products is there. Finding the cure for cancer, diabetes, and other killers as well as preventing other maladies would be good business, domestically as well as globally.

Introducing ways to reduce the costs of health care could be big business here in the U.S. where the cost is a big burden. In addition, the baby boom generation is entering the years where more money is spent on health care than any other time in people's lives. From in-home care and nursing homes to hospitals, biotech, and medical industries should do well.

Leisure and Entertainment

The baby boom generation, and the over fifty generation, is the largest group of people worldwide in the global economy. After health care, leisure and entertainment is what this group wants to spend money on besides helping their kids and grandkids pay for a college education.

This is also the wealthiest group of people in our society, and that means they will be spending money on the things that matter to them now and over the next few decades. Country clubs, cruise lines, resorts, sporting activities, and health and wellness industries should all benefit in the years to come.

Energy

With oil having so many negative side effects as our main energy producer, another inexpensive source of energy would be very welcome worldwide. We do have wind power and solar power as well as corn power.

However, these haven't worked out as we have hoped, although they are part of the overall solution. A breakthrough in an energy supply that is practical and cost efficient with little, if any, negative side effects would certainly be a home run.

Which Growth Tools Work Best?

The reason there are so many different investment tools is because an entire financial industry continues to develop them. Some are good, some are bad, but for the most part, they all try to accomplish pretty much the same thing. They all try to give us some kind of positive return given a certain amount of risk.

The basic idea is that the investment tools that don't have much risk almost always don't give us much return. Likewise, the ones with a lot of risk have a possible high return.

Having gotten that Investment 101 idea out of the way, what it comes down to is which investment tools work the best? In my opinion, the ones that cost the least and that accomplish the highest Financial Wellness goals are the ones that work the best.

Asset class selection

The investment tools that cost the least and meet the financial wellness goals are found through a process called "asset class selection." Asset class selection is the most important determinant of portfolio performance.

Studies have shown that 94% of returns will come from which assets are invested in. Only 2% of returns over time will come from buying and selling at the right time, also known as market timing.

In addition, only 4% of returns will come from buying "underpriced" assets. Trying to find a great deal or trying to time the market is just not a sustainable long-term investment approach.

There are four main types of asset classes that most people deal with in their investment lifetime. They are: real estate, company stocks, bonds, and cash equivalents.

Real Estate

The real estate that most people will invest in during their lives will be in buying and selling their very own homes. Residential real estate has traditionally increased in value at about 3% per year on average that basically keeps up with inflation.

Therefore, a home is not a bad investment for the "security basket" because it does provide slow but relatively steady increase in value and it does give us a place to live. It's not going to give us much bang for our buck as far as a growth investment.

There are many people that invest in real estate and have made a lot of money in the process over time. It definitely can be a growth investment vehicle as well as a capital preservation and income strategy.

There are volumes of books dedicated to investing in real estate. If you are interested in real estate for your growth and preservation baskets, read up on it. Before jumping in yourself, like any investing, it is wise to do your homework before putting actual money to work.

Historically, real estate returns have not been tied to stock market returns, this means they are typically inverse related. Therefore, it has been a good diversification tool for investors that are in the stock market.

Investors can access real estate without having to buy physical property. There are funds that people can trade in the stock market which give them exposure to the real estate market. Real estate partnerships also exist for the more sophisticated investors to participate in.

Stocks

Individual company stocks, exchange traded funds (ETFs) and mutual funds are ways to buy into both domestic and international companies. When you buy a share of stock of a company you actually become one of the owners. Owners participate directly in the growth or decline of the value of the organization.

Individual stocks can be very volatile to invest in and therefore are regarded by most investors as an aggressive growth approach to investing. However, there are blue chip stocks, which are stocks of large companies that have mostly done well over time. These stocks are not considered as volatile and are good investments more for their steady dividend payments rather than for their growth.

ETFs

Exchange traded funds, also known as ETFs offer investors an undivided interest in a pool of stocks, bonds or commodities and thus are similar in many ways to traditional mutual funds, except that shares in an ETF can be bought and sold throughout the day like stocks on a securities exchange.

ETFs generally provide the easy diversification, low expense ratios, tax efficiency, and still maintain all the features of ordinary stock, such as limit orders, short selling, and options. Among the advantages of ETFs are the following:

• *Lower costs* - ETFs generally have lower costs than other investment products because most ETFs are not actively managed, and because ETFs are insulated from the costs of having to buy and sell securities to accommodate shareholder purchases and redemptions. ETFs typically have lower marketing, distribution, and accounting expenses.

• *Buying and selling flexibility* - ETFs can be bought and sold at current market prices at any time during the trading day, unlike mutual funds and unit investment trusts, which can only be traded at the end of the trading day. As publicly traded securities, their shares can be purchased on margin and sold short, enabling the use of hedging strategies, and traded using stop orders and limit orders, which allow investors to specify the price points at which they are willing to trade.

• **_Tax efficiency_** - ETFs generally generate relatively low capital gains, because they typically have low turnover of their portfolio securities. While this is an advantage they share with other index funds, their tax efficiency is further enhanced because they do not have to sell securities to meet investor redemptions.

• **_Market exposure and diversification_** - ETFs provide an economical way to rebalance portfolio allocations and to "equitize" cash by investing it quickly. An index ETF inherently provides diversification across an entire index. ETFs offer exposure to a diverse variety of markets, including broad-based indexes, broad-based international and country-specific indexes, industry sector-specific indexes, bond indexes, and commodities.

• **_Transparency_** - ETFs, whether index funds or actively managed, have transparent portfolios and are priced at frequent intervals throughout the trading day.

```
┌─────────────────────────────────────────┐
│  ┌───────────────────────────────────┐  │
│  │                                   │  │
│  │       Special Note on ETFs:       │  │
│  │                                   │  │
│  │  The main reason I like ETFs and use │
│  │  them in my wealth management     │  │
│  │  business is that they are very low cost │
│  │  and give my clients access to just about │
│  │  any market sector and asset class. │  │
│  │                                   │  │
│  │  For $1, or less, I can buy, or sell, an ETF │
│  │  for a client's portfolio and the annual │
│  │  expense of owning that ETF is a fraction │
│  │  of the cost of owning a mutual fund. │
│  │                                   │  │
│  └───────────────────────────────────┘  │
└─────────────────────────────────────────┘
```

Mutual Funds

A mutual fund is a professionally managed type of collective investment scheme that pools money from many investors and invests typically in investment securities such as stocks, bonds, short-term money market instruments, other mutual funds, other securities, and/or commodities as precious metals. The mutual fund will have a fund manager that buys and sells the fund's investments in accordance with the fund's investment objective.

That is basically all that most people want to know about mutual funds. However, since mutual funds have been such a large part of most investor's portfolios for so many years, it might be interesting to know a little more about them.

The details are a bit mind-boggling, and it's not hard to understand why some mutual funds have gotten to be so expensive for investors to hold. There are so many fees and players involved that the only way costs can go on these funds is up.

The following is some history and some details about mutual funds and the huge industry that has evolved around them. This is not necessarily a good thing for investors.

In the U.S., a fund registered with the Securities and Exchange Commission (SEC) under both SEC and IRS rules must distribute nearly all of its net income and net realized gains from the sale of securities (if any) to its investors at least annually. Most funds are overseen by a board of directors that is charged with ensuring the fund is managed appropriately by its investment adviser and other service organizations and vendors, all in the best interests of the fund's investors.

There are many mutual fund sectors that can be used to accomplish a well-diversified asset allocation strategy. Within each sector there are hundreds of funds to choose from. All in all there are thousands of different mutual funds, and that's too many, if you ask me!

The mutual fund industry appears to be a victim of its own success. Early on when mutual funds were first being developed and offered to the general public, they served a great need of helping people to easily diversify their investments.

At the end of the 1960s, there were approximately 270 funds with $48 billion in assets. The first retail index fund, First Index Investment Trust, was formed in 1976 and headed by John

Bogle, the founder of Vanguard Investments. This mutual fund is now called the Vanguard 500 Index Fund and is one of the world's largest mutual funds, with more than $100 billion in assets.

A key factor in mutual-fund growth was the 1975 change in the Internal Revenue Code that allowed individuals to open individual retirement accounts (IRAs). Even people already enrolled in corporate pension plans could contribute a limited amount (at the time, up to $2,000 a year). Mutual funds are now popular in employer-sponsored "defined-contribution" retirement plans such as 401(k)s and 403(b)s as well as IRAs including Roth IRAs.

As mentioned before, mutual funds enjoyed huge success over the years because they were very easy to get into. For $25, an investor could start investing in a diversified way through a variety of mutual funds.

The financial industry took the bull by the horns and sold investors on the merits of an intelligently-diversified strategy of several mutual funds. Everyone bought into the story that seemed to make sense during the growth era of the 80s and 90s. All one had to do is invest in the S&P Index mutual fund to make money.

There are now approximately 8,000 mutual funds in the United States, with combined assets of $12.356 trillion. Unfortunately, the success of the mutual fund industry has been much more for the companies running them and selling them than for the people actually investing in them.

This has even been true for many investors during the boom years because investors pick the wrong mutual funds trying to beat the market or tried to time it by moving in and out of funds hoping to do better in the short run.

The actual mutual fund managers themselves do not fare much better than the individual investors. Very few fund managers have performed consistently well over time.

Regardless of how mutual funds have performed over the years, they continue to be very popular. There are a couple of reasons for this. First, we are creatures of habit, and it's hard to change old habits, and second mutual funds are very profitable for the companies offering them. Therefore, they're stuck pushing them onto their clients every year.

Cost of Mutual Funds

The fee structure of a mutual fund can be divided into two or three main components: management fee, non-management expense, and 12b-1/non-12b-1 fees.

The management fee for the fund is usually synonymous with the contractual investment advisory fee charged for the management of a fund's investments.

Apart from the management fee, there are certain non-management expenses which most funds must pay. Some of the more significant non-management expenses are: transfer agent expenses (this is usually the person you get on the other end of the phone line when you want to purchase/sell shares of a fund).

Custodian expense (the fund's assets are kept in custody by a bank that charges a custody fee), legal/audit expense, fund accounting expense, registration expense (the SEC charges a registration fee when funds file registration statements with it), board of directors/trustees expense (the members of the board who oversee the fund are usually paid a fee for their time spent at meetings), and printing and postage expense (incurred when printing and delivering shareholder reports).

In the United States, 12b-1 service fees/shareholder servicing fees are contractual fees a fund may charge to cover the marketing expenses of the fund.

The financial advisor handling your account gets paid a fee when you buy into a mutual fund. This can be as little as 1% per year for as long as you own the fund, 5.75% for a one time up front commission, or something in between that has some annual fee plus an up-front commission.

Additionally, funds may charge early redemption fees to discourage investors from swapping money in and out of the fund quickly that may force the fund to make bad trades to obtain the necessary liquidity.

An additional expense that does not pass through the fund's income statement and cannot be controlled by the investor is brokerage commissions. Broker commissions are incorporated into the price of securities bought and sold and, thus, are a component of the gain or loss on investments.

Are Mutual Funds Good For Investors?

A large part of the proliferation of mutual funds is that they are easy to get into. Firms have low initial investment amounts, and the investor can add to the investment in small increments of $25 at a time in some instances.

In this regard, they have been very successful in helping the investor get started and have a professional money manager manage their money. This has been the sales pitch anyway.

Unfortunately for the investor, this has not meant that it's always a good place to put money. The sad fact is that most mutual funds underperform the general market every year.

When the fees are all added up, and we found out earlier there are lots of fees, the investment loses its luster. Investment firms and advisors that promote and use these funds do not tell us this because they are trained to put our money in mutual funds. This is regardless of the fact that most do not return more than one of the index funds that have much lower fees.

To answer the question regarding if mutual funds are good for investors is to say that there are less expensive ways to accomplish the same thing. ETFs provide the same benefits of diversification and ease of use as mutual funds but at lower cost and better tax efficiency.

To summarize our approach in the growth basket, utilizing a proven system that works over time, real estate, individual company stocks, ETFs, and mutual funds have been a great way to add value to a well-diversified portfolio. This growth basket strategy requires an investment approach that is disciplined and has the proper time horizon to work which is typically five years or more.

As assets grow, we will take some of the profits off the table and move them into a safe place so that gains are preserved when they are needed the most.

∞

Chapter 8

Basket #3 – Preservation

This is the basket to preserve the money that has accumulated and grown in the "growth" basket. While maintaining the growth basket over the years, a certain amount of the profits should be put into investments that have a very low chance of going down in value but still have some growth potential.

These types of investments will be found in the preservation basket and can include different types of bonds and bond funds. Some are taxable and some may be non-taxable depending on if the goal is to protect income from a high tax bracket or not.

The main idea of the preservation basket is to accumulate the assets that will be needed as we age. This is especially true if your preservation basket is to fund retirement and sunset years of life. If this is the case, make sure to truly preserve funds so that they will be there when you need them.

This can be accomplished in many different ways. Each one has their own risk-reward relationship just like it did in the growth basket. Typically the investments that have low risk will have a low return.

The inverse is also true, investments that have a higher return typically come with a little more risk. Having said that, none of the true asset preservation products should come with a risk that would move it out of the preservation basket and make it more a of a growth basket investment.

Investment grade bonds are usually associated with this preservation basket. Certificates of deposit are also a popular way to preserve accumulated capital.

Annuities and other insurance products can also be used in the right situation. The problem with annuities is that most come with a high commission to the sales person that many times they are pushed onto the investor when it's not the best thing for them. It's important for clients to get a second and third opinion on annuities and insurance products before making a decision to make sure they are getting good advice in the best interest of the client.

Financial Plan

In order to have a financial plan that works, you must know if you'll have enough money saved up to take out the desired amount of income during retirement years. It's important to have a plan, because like any endeavor, if we fail to plan, we plan to fail. I've seen first-hand the worry and depression that can affect people as they near retirement age, because they don't have a plan.

If financial wellness is important during retirement years, or at any time, then having some kind of a simple plan is a must. This financial plan doesn't have to be elaborate. Sometimes having a simple plan so that we know where we are and where we are headed is enough to give us the knowledge to make decisions and feel like we have control over our financial destiny.

Things to consider in your financial plan:

1. How old are you? (how much time until retirement?)

2. How much money is saved up now?

3. How much will you be receiving from Social Security?

4. How much annual income do you plan on receiving from savings during the retirement years? (Actuaries are now using 90 as the average life span. If retire at age 65, God willing, we may have twenty-five years in retirement that will need to be funded.)

5. What average rate of return are you expecting from investments?

6. At what age do you want to stop working?

Aspects of your plan that you have some control over:

1. How much is saved per day, week, month, and year?

2. Being aggressive or conservative.

3. How long we keep working?

Tools in the Preservation Basket

Bonds

There are many types of bonds, and some have been around for more than one hundred years. Actually, not many people know this, but the bond market is many times larger in dollars traded every year than the stock market.

We just don't hear about the bond market very much because most of the investors in bonds are institutions rather than individuals and since bonds are not as volatile as stocks, they don't make for good T.V. coverage. It's the equivalent of watching the proverbial race between the turtle (bonds) and the hare (stocks). The turtle is not as interesting to watch.

ETFs

We first talked about ETFs in the growth basket and these work just as well in the preservation basket. For the preservation basket, also use them for investing in bond funds.

You can invest in many types of bond funds such as corporate, government, high yield, municipals, mortgage, or all of them at the same time with one ETF. Bond ETFs give us the conservation approach plus diversification within the bond world to spread out the risk.

CDs and Money Market Accounts

These low risk investments are used often in this basket because they pay interest while preserving capital. However, because of their current low return, they are mostly used as a place to "park" cash while waiting to do something else with the money.

Annuities

These insurance industry investments are sold quite aggressively by some insurance and financial advisors mainly because they pay high commissions. Annuities can be good for an investor that wants to ensure a certain income stream for the rest of their lives and for the rest of their spouse's life as well.

The investor just has to be willing to pay for that kind of assurance and that is what makes them somewhat of an expensive investment and/or insurance program. But if the investor is aware of the cost and is still interested in the benefit that they offer, then they are a fine alternative in the preservation basket.

Insurance

Insurance can be used quite effectively in the preservation basket because it offers several ways to protect yourself and your loved ones.

Long-Term Care

Long-term care insurance is good for someone to look at that is between the ages of 55 to 65 because at those ages the premiums are still affordable for most people. What this insurance does is it pays for your care when you become unable to care for yourself.

For instance, when folks cannot get around in their home because of old age or a debilitating disease, they can have an in-home care service take care of them every day if needed. This kind of health care can be expensive, and the insurance pays a daily rate that covers all or the majority of the daily cost.

About 60% of individuals over age 65 will require at least some type of long-term care services during their lifetime. About 40% of those receiving long-term care today are between 18 and 64.

Once a change of health occurs, long-term care insurance may not be available. Early onset (before age 65) Alzheimer's and Parkinson's disease are rare but do occur.

Other benefits of long-term care insurance:

- Many individuals may feel uncomfortable relying on their children or family members for support and find that long-term care insurance could help cover out-of-pocket expenses. Without long-term care insurance, the cost of providing these services may quickly deplete the savings of the individual and/or their family.

- Premiums paid on a long-term care insurance product may be eligible for an income tax deduction. The amount of the deduction depends on the age of the covered person. Benefits paid from a long-term care contract are generally excluded from income.

- Business deductions of premiums are determined by the type of business. Generally corporations paying premiums for an employee are 100% deductible if not included in employee's taxable income.

Disability

Disability insurance, often called DI or disability income insurance, is a form of insurance that insures the person's earned income against the risk that disability will make working (and therefore earning) impossible. It includes paid sick leave, short-term disability benefits, and long-term disability benefits. Statistics show in the U.S. a disabling accident occurs every second.

Our government also provides disability insurance. These Social Security programs provide a floor beneath all the other forms of disability insurance in our country such as workman's compensation insurance.

In other words, they are the safety net that catches everyone who was either (a) otherwise uninsured or (b) otherwise underinsured. As such, they are very large, very important programs, with many beneficiaries. The general theory of the benefit formula is that the benefit is not large but is enough to prevent abject poverty.

Protecting Wealth – Things to Think About:

- Life insurance
    - What do you want for your family if you died today?
    - Generally during working years you want seven to ten times annual income.

- Long Term Care insurance
    - Do you have parents in need, or have you considered your own need?

- Disability insurance
    - What would happen to your other goals if you had to use your own savings for a disability?
    - Do you have another way to provide income for your family if you became disabled?

Transferring Wealth – Things to Think About:

- Do you have a will or family trust?

- Do you need to update your will?

- Who will act as guardian of your children?

- Are your beneficiary designations current?

- If you own a business, what are your succession plans?

> "The gain of about 30 years in life expectancy in developed countries stands out as one of the most important accomplishments in the 20th century."
>
> James W. Vaupel

So You Want to Live to 100?

- A child born after the year 2000 is likely to live to be a hundred years-old and will live a healthier life in old age than previous generations.

- The implications are enormous for everything from retirement planning to health care costs.

- Life expectancy now is on average eighty-five-years-old (low 80s for men and high 80s for women).

- If you add another fifteen years on top of that, then people need to become much more knowledgeable about saving and investing for retirement.

- Less than 20% of Americans in their 50s has even tried to design a retirement plan.

Social Security

- Under the current U.S. Social Security system, the "normal" retirement age is defined as 65.

- When Social Security was put in place in the 1930s, life expectancy was a lot shorter. We adopted the "normal" retirement age of 65 from the German system. In those days, half the people never lived that long.

- Was originally designed to only cover those who outlived their life expectancy.

- "If we are to finance longer life spans, we will have to train smarter, work longer, save more for our retirement, and restructure Social Security as the longevity insurance program it was intended to be." Olivia Mitchell, Professor of Insurance and Risk Management., Wharton.

∞

Chapter 9

Basket #4 – Fulfillment

In this basket live your lives to the fullest. In your fulfillment of life you aren't concerned about financial security and growth because you've already taken care of that.

In this basket relax and do the things that really matter to you. However, you really only can do this to its greatest potential if you've done the beginning steps of taking care of basic needs and grown assets to the point where you can reap the benefits of hard work and discipline.

Do you have to wait till retirement before being fulfilled? No, you can certainly enjoy fulfillment all along your journey to financial wellness. Your happiness depends upon a balanced life, and that includes taking the time during the security, growth and preservation stages to live a fulfilling life.

All stages have their aspects of a fulfilling life and the events that lead to fulfillment weave themselves in and out of our lives along the way. Financial Wellness is really about having the resources necessary to finance choices so that you can follow through with what you want to do.

When you stop working later in life, this is when you want to have the preservation basket overflowing to finance the fulfillment in retirement years. Life in retirement could be a long time, and the quality of our retirement years could depend greatly on the resources that have accumulated in the preservation basket up to this point.

A typical person retiring at sixty-five and living to eighty-five is living twenty years in retirement. The preservation basket will be at its most full level during retirement years, and that works out perfectly, because that is when you'll be withdrawing the most and for the longest period of time.

Life expectancy in our country continues to increase. This is good news in that it allows us to live longer and healthier lives. There is so much that we can accomplish that can bring so much fulfillment to our lives when we are older.

This is because we typically do not have the responsibility of raising a family and of working to make a living when we are older. By having a healthy preservation basket to finance the sunset years, we take a lot of worry out of our lives and can focus on things that really matter to us.

If I asked 100 people what their idea of fulfillment would look like I'd probably get 100 different answers. Fulfillment is very personal and it will be different for everyone which is what makes life interesting. This is not a cookie cutter approach nor should it be.

We want to be as creative as we want, be true to ourselves, and be passionate about what we do in life. Having said that, I've listed what I think are some common themes of what a life of fulfillment might include in our western modern day culture.

Time and Work Freedom

Hopefully by now our philosophy of wealth includes the idea that money won't make us happy. However, the freedom to make decisions about how we spend our time has the potential to make us happy.

For example, being able to work part-time instead of full time can make us happy. Or, the ability to not work at all outside the home, so we can take care of our children or an elderly parent can bring us lots of fulfillment. This could be for either a stay-at-home mom or dad.

I know because my wife stayed home for ten years while our children were young, and I know that we are very happy that she was able to do that. Now she's able to return to the workforce because the kids don't need a parent at home all day anymore.

In some cases, as we grow older and have accumulated a certain amount of resources, we can feel confident enough to semi-retire. This often means that we still have lots of energy and can contribute at work, but we also want to devote significant time to other hobbies and interests.

Having work freedom can also include taking the opportunity to be a business owner. I know from my own experience that this can be quite fulfilling because I like managing my own schedule. However, I know others that are fulfilled working for someone else. It is having the option to choose that can bring happiness.

Goals and Dreams

We all have our goals and dreams that we think will be part of bringing us fulfillment in life. This is a good thing! Our goals and dreams make life worth living.

Sometimes after accomplishing a lifelong dream, we realize that we're ready for another one. I think the right attitude here is to try as many things out as we can in the time that we've been given.

Here is a list below of some possible goals and dreams to get us thinking of some ideas. If you already have a list of your own, that's even better. Remember, we can always change our goals. Stay flexible.

- Retirement
    - Want to retire early?
    - Want to travel?
    - How about volunteer work?
    - Do you want to spend a great deal of time with children and grandchildren?
    - Do you have an idea how much money you need to retire?

- Education
    - How many people are you planning to help?
    - How much would you like to contribute?
    - Do you know what it would cost?
    - How about advanced degrees for yourself?

- Vacation home
    - Where would you like your second home to be?

- How far away from your main home?
- What kind of home is it?
- What will it cost?
- Is this a starter vacation home or the big dream vacation home?

- Buying or starting a business
  - What kind of business?
  - How much time do you want to devote?
  - What experience or advantage do you have?
  - What are your expectations?

- Real estate investments
  - Rental property?
  - Land for development?
  - Speculation?

- Lump sum of money for whatever you want
  - Vacations?
  - Luxuries?
  - Bigger house?

Choices in Retirement

Financial Wellness is all about having the power to make choices in the quality of our retirement. Some of us are going to want a quiet and relatively simple retirement because we've been very busy and traveling while we worked. Others are going to want a very active retirement with perhaps some around-the-world travel and adventures with some occasional stopping in to visit the grandkids. And, of course, most people will settle in somewhere in between.

I know that having a permanent home somewhere close to family and then having a second home in an opposite climate has been a favorite for many folks in retirement. Florida and Arizona have become the second home for many retirees from northern states.

Europe seems to be a playground and popular destination for some as well. Latin America continues to be a favorite for folks who want to experience a very different culture but where most people can speak English and not be too far from home.

There seems to be no end to the choices that are available to us during these years when we don't have so many responsibilities. In addition, this period of life may be longer for us than any such period throughout history.

Charity and Contribution

The feeling of being significant in the world is a powerful sentiment that drives us and motivates us. That's one reason we work so hard in our careers, so that we get that feeling of accomplishment of having done something important with our lives. This same feeling of being significant doesn't only have to come from our career, it can also come from serving and helping others.

In addition to feeling good about ourselves when we volunteer, support good causes, and join service organizations, we also make a huge impact on the lives of many others. Therefore, charity and contribution in our lives can really be quite fulfilling and therefore an important part of our overall financial wellness.

There is no shortage of ways to help out. We can help with our time, treasure and/or our talents. Our service can be local or international. It can be during our working hours such as volunteering through the organization we work for, or it can be on our own time.

We can make it a regular hobby, or we can devote only a few minutes at a time. There are literally hundreds of ways that being charitable can be a part of our lives. The return on this investment is worth many times any amount measured by money.

Being charitable is also something that sets our country apart from others in the world. In my travels, I have never witnessed as much giving as I have in the U.S.

We seem to be quick to lend a helping hand without much thought. We understand that helping people is something that we can do without much trouble. We can make a difference. It's part of our culture.

For example, my mother-in-law who is from Panama served as the Minister of Education a few years ago. She had a chance meeting with an American at an airport during one of her trips abroad. This man found out about her position in the government, and offered to send to her department some care baskets with baby supplies for distribution among the poor on behalf of his religious organization here in the states.

She was impressed by his offer of generosity on the spot but didn't give it much thought when she returned home from her trip. Not long afterward, her office received hundreds of care baskets from this man's organization. Needless to say, she was very impressed by the generosity and arranged to have them distributed to poor mothers in need.

About ten years ago, I had the opportunity to be a part of a charity that continues today to help children from poor countries stay in school. My idea was that if these needy children stayed in school, that the cycle of poverty would be broken.

Otherwise, many of these kids only go to school for a few years. When they are old enough to work they are taken out of school and that is the end as far as a formal education was concerned.

As we all know, the more education a person has the better income they can earn, the higher standard of living they can enjoy, and the better citizens they can become.

This charity has other positive results as well that affect all of us indirectly. These children will grow up to be part of the success of their own towns, cities, countries.

Hopefully they now feel that they are part of the overall success of the world. This interconnectedness that we all share should lead to a more peaceful place here on earth.

We all have our own motivations, our own backgrounds, and our own abilities as to why we are a giving nation and a giving people. I think that we all can agree that a big part of being fulfilled is having the feeling that we are making the world a better place, even if it is just one person at a time.

This is one reason that it's important for all of us to be individually financial well. It's important because if we can take care of the money part of our lives, than it opens us up to other more fulfilling areas to explore.

In other words, if we are worrying about money all the time, we won't be thinking about how we can contribute. And if we don't have the time or resources to participate in these higher level endeavors, then who will?

The opportunity to extend outward from ourselves and make a positive impact in other people's experience of life is truly gratifying and fulfilling. Therefore, we don't want to miss out on these parts of life simply because we haven't gotten our personal finances in order.

Andrew Carnegie created a fortune in the late 1800's and early 1900's in steel. He was a self-made billionaire, and probably the world's first. As a child, he was an immigrant to the U.S. from Scotland.

He grew up poor and worked in the steel mills of Pennsylvania. However, he loved learning and working and eventually grew to own many steel mills in the industrialist era of our country. He was a peace-maker and even attempted to stop the beginning of WWI by offering to pay Germany, out of his own pocket, not to go to war.

Before his death, Carnegie gave away hundreds of millions and is most famous for funding the free library system that Americans have enjoyed ever since. He was also a philanthropist in England and back in his native country of Scotland.

After his death in 1919, the rest of his fortune was given away to worthy causes by the foundations he created. Ever heard of Carnegie Hall? The following was from a speech that he gave quoting from the book "The Gospel of Wealth."

"This, then, is held to be the duty of the man of wealth: first, to set an example of modest unostentatious living, shunning display; to provide moderately for the legitimate wants of those dependent upon him; and, after doing so, to consider all surplus revenues which come to him simply as trust funds which he is strictly bound as a matter of duty to administer in the manner which, in his judgment, is best calculated to produce the most beneficial results for the community."

"God's Team, Making the World Better One Person at a Time."

2009

James Bresnahan

Is There An Easier Way?

We can't take a short cut and jump from basket #1 to basket #4. It would be nice to do, but it doesn't work that way. In fact, there are people that have won the lottery and ended up broke because they had not learned the skills in the growth and preservation baskets.

Since they did not build the good habits that we learn in these baskets, they did not have the ability to "grow" and "preserve" their good fortune and lost it in the end. Therefore, like many things in life, we are much better off taking the time to go through each of the steps to reach fulfillment and overall financial wellness.

The question, "Is there an easier way?" brings to mind the fable of "The Ant and the Grasshopper." This ancient and time-tested tale was first told by Aesop of Greece more than 2,500 years ago. I remember reading it to my kids when they were young.

The story concerns a grasshopper that spent the warm summer months singing away and playing his violin while the ant worked to store up food for the coming winter. The grasshopper would tell the ants to stop working so hard and enjoy the nice weather.

During the autumn months, the grasshopper continued to ridicule the ants for working so hard instead of relaxing as he was doing. When winter arrives, the snow begins to fall, and the wind begins to blow. The grasshopper finds itself dying of hunger, and upon asking the ant for food and shelter is only rebuked for its idleness.

The ant and his family eventually feel sorry for the freezing and hungry grasshopper and let him in out of the cold to share their food. The ants give him a chair to sit in by the roaring fire, a blanket to put around his shoulders, and a bucket of warm water for his feet. They also give him a hot bowl of soup as the ants sing and dance the night away in their cozy home as the snowstorm rages outside.

The story, of course, is used to teach the virtues of hard work and saving, and the perils of not doing so. It is as true today as it was back in ancient Greece. There is no substitute for diligence.

Chapter 10

Financial Education Section

It is not necessary for our financial wellness to know and understand all the different kinds of investment tools that the financial industry uses to manage our money. However, for the reader inclined or curious as to what these tools are it can be interesting to learn about them. The following section is an introduction to some common methods of investment that are available:

Target Date Funds

Target date funds are sometimes promoted as a good first point of entry into investing. Why? Because these funds take into consideration the client's investment horizon and personal risk/return profile. They also automatically reallocate the fund as needed to keep the important targeted mix of stocks, bonds, and cash.

The idea of these target date mutual funds is that it makes investing very simple. Basically, they want you to pick a year of retirement. Then put money into the corresponding target fund. That is very easy to do and the idea is to forget about it, and money will grow.

One huge selling point is that the fund will automatically adjust the mix of growth and preservation type funds over time. In other words, as we grow older and we get closer to that target retirement date, the fund will automatically have more preservation investments and less growth investments.

This all sounds great, right? However, the problem is that these funds are not managed by anyone in particular or with much attention. Therefore, the returns are not very good because they tend to be overly conservative. They also do poorly in consolidation cycles like we are in now.

So as investors in these target funds, what we gain in ease of use, we lose in a good return. I have a hard time encouraging my clients to use these for that exact reason. There are better ways to invest for the long-term which will have better returns with commensurate levels of risk taking.

Lifestyle Funds

Lifestyle funds are not much better than target date funds as you can see in the graph (**next page**). This is the Fidelity 60/40 fund with symbol FSAAX as an example. It's comprised of approximately 60% equities and 40% bonds. This fund in particular has a front end fee of 5.75% that is paid to the broker for selling you the fund.

In addition, there's a 1% annual fee for managing the fund every year that is taken out of the investors account balance. The dark line is the 60/40 fund and the light line is the market in general represented here by the S&P500.

This balanced fund of 60/40 split is a growth strategy for older middle-aged investors because the majority of the investments are still in stocks. This investor has many years ahead of them before retirement and has the time to grow the funds.

Since bonds did better during this period from September 2008 to July 2010, this fund out-performed the stock market because it has 40% of the funds invested in bonds. This is an example of tactical investing in that certain sectors do better than others at different times. Therefore, it is good to have some diversity and flexibility in the management of the funds.

As investors age into a more conservative approach a 40/60 split fund is recommended. That is a 40% exposure to the "growth basket" with stocks and 60% to the "preservation basket" with bonds.

The graph shows the FTAWX (**on next page**) that with less stocks and with more bonds that the return was higher, which isn't the usual case. This is because bonds were a majority of the holdings during this bad time for stocks.

The investment over this very volatile two-year period has not returned much in growth but did have a positive return if held for the period. In addition, the volatility was much lower because the 60% in bonds brought stability.

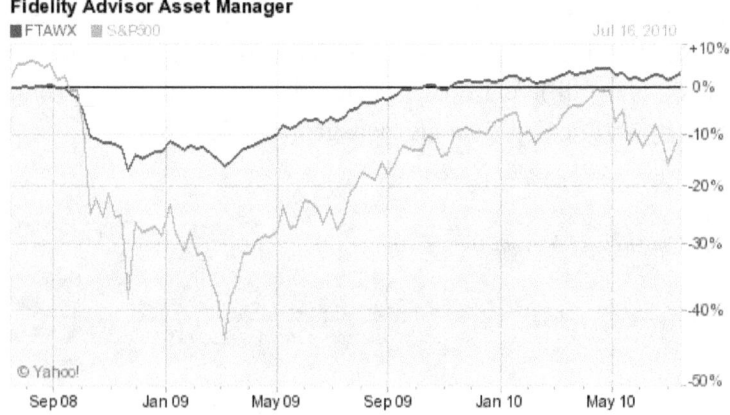

Fidelity Advisor Asset Manager

The next graph (**on next page**) shows how an approximate 100% bond investment performed over the same two-year period. The difference is quite dramatic when you can see it on a graph like this. The investment remained in positive territory most of the time which is what is important in the "preservation basket." This bond fund example, with symbol FVIAX, is comprised of U.S. government and agency bonds that contain little risk.

If an investor were to buy this fund through a financial advisor firm, they might pay an up-front sales charge of 4% plus an *annual fee* of .77% to Fidelity for managing the fund. This fund did return on average 6% per year over the last decade which is consistent with what can be expected for a bond fund.

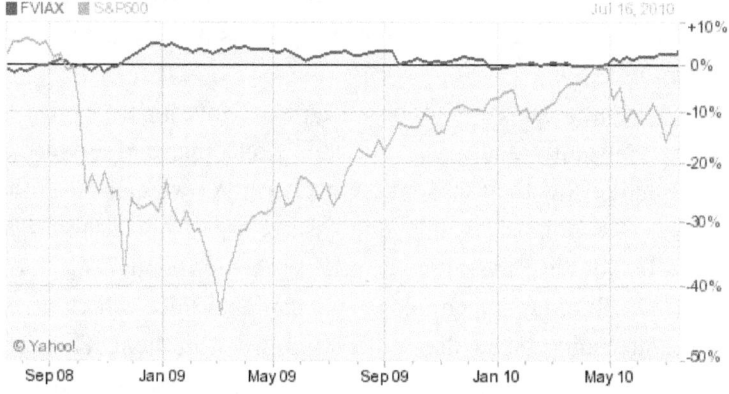

Fidelity Advisor Government Inc

FVIAX   S&P500   Jul 16, 2010

Sep 08   Jan 09   May 09   Sep 09   Jan 10   May 10

Professional Money Managers

Using professional money managers for all or a part of a client's portfolio can be a very rewarding strategy. The key is to identify money managers with consistent good performance without taking on outsized risk.

Usually the better money managers have a disciplined investment approach and a consistent style they utilize. The goal of these managers is to outperform the average stock market return above and beyond the fee they charge their clients.

It's important that these money managers also have their own personal investments working right alongside the client's money. That way, it's obvious that the manager is doing everything possible to keep risk under control and the strategy sound.

I have personally had great returns using a money manager, and this is what I do for my clients as well. Taking an active role on a daily basis and using systems that work has been very good to me.

Money can be made in all types of investment cycles if we are constantly analyzing and acting on opportunities in the world markets as they present themselves. As we can see from the previous graphs, even if one asset class is not doing well (domestic equities) there may be others that are (bonds).

With today's technology, we can determine which asset classes are doing better than others and invest in them. This can be done quite effectively and inexpensively compared to a few years ago. Technology has really leveled the playing field for money managers with no need for research staff.

A trade at a traditional big name investment firm will cost a client a minimum of $75. The reason the big firms charge that much is to pay for the overhead of secretaries, sales managers, office buildings, advertising, and professional athlete endorsements.

Compare that to a trade with an efficient high-tech online broker at $1.00. Needless to say, I use the online method for my clients.

Benchmarks

A stock market index is a method of measuring a section of the stock market. Many indices are cited by news or financial services firms and are used as benchmarks to measure the performance of portfolios. The following are some popular ways that we compare our individual returns to the general markets around the world:

S&P 500

The S&P 500 stock market index is maintained by Standard & Poor's and comprises 500 large American companies covering about 75% of the American stock market by capitalization. In other words, it shows the general valuation on a daily basis of 500 of the largest companies in the U.S.

In effect, it takes the pulse of the heartbeat of our domestic stock market. It is one of the main indexes that we track, or benchmark against that gives us an idea of how we are doing regarding our own investment performance.

Dow Jones Industrial Average

The Dow Jones Industrial Average, also referred to as the Industrial Average, the Dow Jones, the Dow 30, or simply the Dow, is one of several stock market indices created by *Wall Street Journal* editor and Dow Jones & Company co-founder, Charles Dow. The average is named after Dow and one of his business associates, statistician Edward Jones.

It is an index that shows how thirty large, publicly owned companies based in the United States have traded during a standard trading session in the stock market. It is the second oldest U.S. market index after the Dow Jones Transportation Average, which Dow also created.

The *Industrial* portion of the name is largely historical, as many of the modern thirty components have little or nothing to do with traditional heavy industry. The average is price-weighted, and to compensate for the effects of stock splits and other adjustments, it's currently a scaled average.

The value of the Dow is not the actual average of the prices of its component stocks, but rather the sum of the component prices divided by a divisor. The divisor changes whenever one of the component stocks has a stock split or stock dividend, so as to generate a consistent value for the index.

Along with the NASDAQ Composite, the S&P 500 Index, and the Russell 2000 Index, the Dow is among the most closely-watched benchmark indices tracking targeted stock market activity. Although Dow compiled the index to gauge the performance of the industrial sector within the American economy, the index's performance continues to be influenced by not only corporate and economic reports, but also by domestic and foreign political events such as war and terrorism, as well as by natural disasters that could potentially lead to economic harm.

MSCI World

The MSCI World is a stock market index of 1,500 'world' stocks. It is maintained by MSCI Inc., formerly Morgan Stanley Capital International, and is often used as a common benchmark for 'world' or 'global' stock funds.

The index includes a collection of stocks of all the developed markets in the world, as defined by MSCI. The index includes securities from twenty-four countries but excludes stocks from emerging and frontier economies making it less worldwide than the name suggests.

MSCI Emerging Markets

The MSCI Emerging Markets Index is a free float-adjusted market capitalization index that is designed to measure equity market performance in the global emerging markets. The index represents companies within these countries that are available to investors worldwide.

As of May 2010, MSCI Barra classified the following twenty-one countries as emerging markets:

-  Brazil
- Chile
- China
- Colombia
- Czech Republic
- Egypt
- Hungary
- India
- Indonesia
- Malaysia
- Mexico
- Morocco
- Peru
- Philippines
- Poland
- Russia
- South Africa
- South Korea
- Taiwan
- Thailand
- Turkey

Individual Bonds

Bonds are a great way to contribute income to an investment portfolio because they are inversely related to some factors that drive company stock values. Therefore, for our purposes of achieving financial wellness, bonds fit into the preservation basket the best. This is because, in general, bonds are a conservative asset that should be utilized as people age for the stability and income that older investors require.

Bonds and stocks are both securities, but the major difference between the two is that stockholders have an equity stake in the company (i.e., they are owners), whereas bondholders have a creditor stake in the company (i.e., they are lenders). Another difference is that bonds usually have a defined term, or maturity, after which the bond is redeemed, whereas stocks may be outstanding indefinitely. Bonds are issued by public authorities, credit institutions, and companies.

Types of Bonds

Below are some of the more common types of individual bonds that are available to investors:

• Fixed rate bonds have a coupon that remains constant throughout the life of the bond.

• Zero-coupon bonds pay no regular interest. They are issued at a substantial discount to par value, so that the interest is effectively rolled up to maturity (and usually taxed as such). The bondholder receives the full principal amount on the redemption date. An example of zero coupon bonds is Series E savings bonds issued by the U.S. government.

• Inflation linked bonds, in which the principal amount and the interest payments are indexed to inflation. The interest rate is normally lower than for fixed-rate bonds with a comparable maturity. However, as the principal amount grows, the payments increase with inflation. Treasury Inflation-Protected Securities (TIPS) and I-bonds are examples of inflation linked bonds issued by the U.S. government.

• Asset-backed securities are bonds whose interest and principal payments are backed by underlying cash flows from other assets. Examples of asset-backed securities are mortgage-backed securities (MBS's), collateralized mortgage obligations (CMOs) and collateralized debt obligations (CDOs).

• Municipal bonds are issued by a state, U.S. Territory, city, local government, or their agencies. Interest income received by holders of municipal bonds is often exempt from the federal income tax and from the income tax of the state in which

122

they are issued, although municipal bonds issued for certain purposes may not be tax exempt.

•   Revenue bond is a special type of municipal bond distinguished by its guarantee of repayment solely from revenues generated by a specified revenue-generating entity associated with the purpose of the bonds. Revenue bonds are typically "non-recourse," meaning that in the event of default, the bondholder has no recourse to other governmental assets or revenues.

Negatives of Bond Investing

•   Bond prices can become volatile depending on the credit rating of the issuer. For instance, if the credit rating agencies upgrade or downgrade the credit rating of the issuer; this will affect the market price.

•   A company's bondholders may lose much or all their money if the company goes bankrupt.

•   Fixed-rate bonds are subject to interest rate risk, meaning that their market prices will decrease in value when the generally prevailing interest rates rise. When the market interest rate rises, the market price of bonds will fall, reflecting investor's ability to get a higher interest rate on their money elsewhere. Note that this drop in the bond's market price does not affect the interest payments to the bondholder at all, so long-term investors who want a specific amount at the maturity date need not worry about price swings in their bonds and do not suffer from interest rate risk.

∞

Chapter 11

Financial Wellness Section

This special section has some concepts for us to think about as we travel down the road toward our personal **Financial Wellness**. These ideas should make the journey easier, more successful, and more fun.

What Determines Our Income?

The answers to these three questions below will tell us a lot about the level of income we can expect to receive from our chosen line of work:

1. **How good are we at what we do?**
2. **What is the demand for what we do?**
3. **How easy is it to replace us?**

I am going to use extreme examples below of career choices to make my point. Of course, most of us will fall somewhere in between these two extreme professions. However, examples serve to help us think about our choices and hopefully help us make better decisions.

Let's take an example of a "good" (#1 from our list of questions) elevator operator who works in a tall office building in downtown New York. By the way, that is the last time I saw an actual elevator operator. It was during my last visit to New York when I checked into a Manhattan hotel.

Sure enough, there he was, pushing the elevator buttons for me. I was amused, because it's not something most of us are used to seeing these days.

So that should give us our first clue as to the "demand" (#2 from our list of questions) for elevator operators, right? There are not many positions needing to be filled all over the country for this type of work.

Now this person might be very good, but honestly, how long do you think it took to train this person to do their job? Maybe an hour to get most of the basics? The only problem is that no matter how good he became at operating the elevator he could be replaced (#3 question from our list) in a matter of minutes.

Let's look at the complete other end of the career spectrum to evaluate what being a good brain surgeon might be like in the same great city of New York. I've never had brain surgery but from what I understand it's very complicated work.

A brain surgeon has had to attend a minimum of eight years of formal training. Not to mention a few more years specializing on the brain. So anywhere from eight to twelve years of school has been completed to reach the level where this doctor can conduct brain surgery.

Now let's use our list to find out if brain surgeons will likely earn a good living. Let's consider that after all the training this doctor is pretty good at what they do. I would also suggest that the demand for this type of surgery is fairly good because people do have severe head injuries, aneurisms, cancers, severe and chronic headaches, and other serious brain problems that need immediate attention.

Our next question is how easy is it to replace this doctor? Well, everybody knows that looking forward to attending years of difficult classes after graduating from high school isn't an easy thing to do. Not many people are willing to put that much time and money into getting ready for their career.

The end result is that there are not many brain surgeons. They aren't easy to replace, and the demand for ones that have a high success rate is, well, high!

In our comparison between these two extreme careers, it's easy to see why elevator operators and brain surgeons earn vastly different amounts from their work. They are both fine individuals, and they both do a great job at what they do, but one earns much more in one year than the other person could possibly earn in a lifetime.

Our path to financial wellness is in many ways very similar to the preceding example. We have choices to make. More than likely none of the choices in themselves are going to determine our whole level of financial wellness over a lifetime.

However, little choices add up and taken together certainly can impact our life. What we want is to make those little choices that are going to get us closer to our **Financial Wellness** goals.

Levels of Abundance

Having a good attitude about money is one of those little choices that can make a huge impact on a person's financial outcome. A big part of having the right financial attitude is how we perceive abundance in our lives.

Abundance and wealth are very much a feeling as lack and scarcity are. They are just the opposite sides of the same coin. We make a choice as to which side to focus our attention on.

Abundance can be:

1. A feeling of being more prosperous.
2. A feeling of having great relationships and many friends.
3. A feeling of love for others and being loved back.

If you agree with my list above, then you are probably like me in thinking that financial wellness has a lot more to do about how we perceive wealth and less about the actual number of dollars in the bank.

Speaking about our perception of wealth and abundance, I've broken down the feelings of abundance into four levels. As you read through the list, try and pin point on what level you are living most of the time. Of course, we experience all of these levels of abundance at different times and at different degrees, but there is one that probably dominates our frame of mind most of the time.

The idea of this exercise is to be aware of what level of abundance we are on most of the time. If we are not satisfied with that level, then we can take steps to move up to the next level. **Financial Wellness** involves keeping a balance between taking care of ourselves and taking care of others as well.

128

The idea is that we can help the poor much better if we aren't poor ourselves. By poor I mean financially, spiritually, physically and emotionally. Here is the list below and I will discuss each level in detail at the end of the list:

Level #1 Abundance:

1. There is only a certain amount. There isn't enough to go around.
2. I "expect" certain benefits and a certain income.
3. I have a "right" to work and to make money. (working is not a basic human right; working is a privilege).
4. Demanding money and a certain lifestyle.

Level #2 Abundance:

1. If I help enough people get what they want, then I'll get what I want.
2. Bartering my time for a financial return – work for a living.
3. If we don't get what we want pretty soon, we'll stop giving and move on to something else.

Level #3 Abundance:

1. I attract good things into my life by the way I live.
2. Serving and adding value whether I get anything back or not.
3. Trusting that someday in its own way and in its own time, the good I do now will benefit someone.

Level #4 Abundance:

1. Serving and adding value even when it is painful.
2. We don't want anything for ourselves.

3. Complete self-sacrifice for the good of others.

Wealth begins and ends in the mind! What we think about comes about! Whether we think we can, or we think we can't, we are exactly right!

What all these statements have in common is that we are responsible for our own outcomes and fulfillment. Take a look at these four levels of abundance to have a better understanding of where you might be on a personal level right now:

Level #1: This is characterized as a *"scarcity"* mentality or egocentric. We demand abundance and are competitive in nature and envious of others. Egocentric is all about what we don't have. The thinking is all about us.

Obviously, this is not where you want to be living. This doesn't sound very financially well, does it? I don't think so either. Let's move on and find out what the other levels are like.

Level #2: This is characterized as a *"bartering"* mentality or ethnocentric. We feel wealthy only if the world is giving us rewards that we feel we deserve from our efforts. If I do a good job for my employer, then I should get a good income and be treated well at work.

Ethnocentrics look at everything in relation to their own culture, language, and customs which they think is centrally the most important. This can lead to pride, vanity, beliefs of one's own group's superiority, and contempt for outsiders.

Level #3: This is characterized as an "attraction" mentality or world centric. At this level, we feel pretty good about ourselves and the world around us.

We are grounded, centered, in the flow of life, and we are happy with all areas of our lives such as our friends, family, and work. We do good things principally because we feel content about who we are and the world around us, not because we expect anything in return.

I would say that most of us have experienced many times level 3 abundance. This is the level that we aspire to and use as a target.

If we could live life at this level all the time then we would feel like we are completely fulfilled. Who could ask for anything more?

Level #4: This is characterized as a *"total abundance"* mentality or spirit centric. At this level, we feel wealthy and prosperous no matter what's going on around us. Our world could be falling apart, at least from others' perspective, but we are existing fully fulfilled through it anyway.

This is a feeling of abundance at its finest. I think we all aspire to this level even though we may not ever feel we can get here. This is when we have to rely on our spiritual nature. Our spirit is capable of reaching this level of abundance and we probably have to become more spiritual to sustain this level.

This does not mean that we have to go to church more often although it may involve that. It means that we need to quiet ourselves more so that our spirit can have a chance to express itself. This could involve spending more time in nature, reading inspirational books, or serving others.

We could also become more spiritual by traveling around the world to marvel at the creation and the different perspectives. I suspect spirituality has a lot to do with giving up our ego, pride, arrogance, humbling ourselves and finding some sort of contribution that is meaningful. Finding our connectedness with people and nature has the potential to make us feel more abundant and content.

The News

Folks, the financial news channels on T.V. for the most part are chatter and try to make investing a sensational sport. This is not what investing is and will not lead us to the kind of financial wellness I'm talking about.

Television and newspapers exist to sell advertising. That is their business. So the more entertaining and sensational they can make the news, the more viewers and readers they will attract, and the more advertising they can sell.

Some of the information is useful, however, it can become a source of too much information. Usually we can't do anything about the news anyway, and this can lead to stress and frustration. Stress in our lives is not going to help us reach financial peace.

The main reason I wrote this book is to help us take a common sense approach to our personal financial lives so that it works for us. If our money management makes sense then we won't worry about it. If we are not worried about our financial lives, then we have probably achieved our goal.

I am grateful for this opportunity to share some insights with you, and I hope they are of some benefit. Many years of **Financial Wellness** is my wish for you and your family!

I am ending this book on achieving **Financial Wellness** with one of my favorite quotes from the great Benjamin Franklin. I hope you will find truth in it as much as I do!

"There are two ways of being happy. We may either diminish our wants or augment our means, either will do, the result is the same; and it is for each man to decide for himself, and do that habit which happens to be the easiest. If you are either sick or poor, however hard it may be to diminish your wants, it will be harder to augment your means. If you are active and prosperous, or young, or in good health, it may be easier for you to augment your means than to diminish your wants.

"But if you are wise, you will do both at the same time, young or old, rich or poor, sick or well; and if you are very wise, you will do both in such a way as to augment the general happiness of society."

Benjamin Franklin

Financial Wellness Community

Subscribe to James' blog to receive **Financial Wellness** on a continuous basis. This is a great way to stay engaged, continue to learn, and comment on money making and investment ideas directly with the author and the community.

Book Orders

This book is a great gift for family members, friends, co-workers, and employees that would appreciate a fresh perspective on personal financial management.

Wealth Management

James is in the business of ideas and making money for people. As a registered investment advisor and professional money manager, he can help you with personal investments, estate and retirement planning, and business accounting, using the **Financial Wellness** method discussed in this book.

Seminars

James has developed seminars that educate audiences on several **Financial Wellness** topics. Please contact him for a list of seminars, fees, and available dates.

www.ingramcontent.com/pod-product-compliance
Lightning Source LLC
Chambersburg PA
CBHW051535170526
45165CB00002B/743